FEAR NO EVIL

Overcoming Our Fears in order to Win the World, and Fulfill Our Divine Destiny

BY

CLAY BROOKS

Clay Brooks
104 Stonington Drive,
Brandon, MS 39047

Unless otherwise indicated, all Scripture quotations in this book are from the New American Standard Version of the Bible.

Front cover design by Gustave Dore, 19th century, from alamy.com, all rights secured.

ACKNOWLEDGMENTS

I want to thank my wife, Anita, and my daughter, Ruth, for their hours of help with editing. If you find any mistakes remaining, they are mine and not theirs. I'd also like to thank my sons Elijah and Isaac for their input and help. I could not have done it without you.

I would like to dedicate this book, first of all, to my Lord Jesus Christ who took all my fears upon Himself and defeated them on the cross so that I could be set free and enjoy His peace.

I would also like to dedicate it to my parents, Pat and Bebe Brooks. They are in heaven now, but they are still my greatest examples of overcoming fear that I know personally. Even though they both were struck with the dreaded disease of polio in their teens, they didn't allow the fears of the future and polio to stop them from living full and rewarding lives. They faced their fears, overcame them, and went on to be an inspiration to all who knew them.

CONTENTS

INTRODUCTION

Terror, panic, distress, uncertainty, fear, and worry are all words that more and more characterize the people and the world we live in. People are struggling with fears and worry at dramatically increasing rates. A new survey (March 2015) by Gallup reports that the number of Americans who worry "a great deal" about a terrorist attack occurring on our home soil climbed 12 points from 2014. That puts it at 51 percent at this time. Concerns about racism and racial problems are up 11 points to 28 percent. Fear over illegal immigration also increased by 6 percent. People are worried about health care and the economy as well. Police officers are being assassinated openly on our streets. Christians are concerned about Supreme Court judgments on moral issues that could threaten their freedom and tax-exempt status. We see our freedoms being taken away at alarming rates. People are fearful of what the future might hold.

The dictionary says that fear is a distressing emotion aroused by impending danger, evil, pain, etc. whether the threat is real or imagined. Fear and worry are things that we all have to deal with in life. Fear is one of the ultimate enemies that will confront us for sure. As long as we are on this earth, until Jesus comes, we'll have to deal with fear. How we deal with it is the question. Jesus can truly set us free from the torment of fear and worry. But we have to follow His instructions if we ever hope to overcome these enemies in this life.

Another thing we may not realize is God's attitude toward cowardice in relation to following Jesus. In **Revelation 21:8** it says that the cowardly are the first ones thrown into the lake of fire. This is one of the reasons that I believe God had me to write this book. God doesn't want His people to be fearful or cowardly. He has given us grace and weapons to be the most courageous and intrepid people on earth.

Over and over throughout the Bible, we see God, angels and Jesus exhorting and encouraging us to "fear not." God's will for us, and part of our inheritance in Christ is that we can live free from fear and worry, and maintain victory over them. Therefore understanding fear and knowing how to deal with it is of utmost importance if we are to have an overcoming Christian life and enjoy the peace that God has planned for us. This is especially true during these end-time "birth pangs" in which we are living today (**Mt. 24**). Actually we may be beyond the birth pangs by now.

When I was a young Christian, God had helped me to face and defeat many fears. I grew up in the Mississippi Delta, and my evangelistic training ground had been going to white and also black barrooms, or "juke joints" as we called them, in order to share the gospel. I had gone into these areas under the compulsion of the Holy Spirit to share Jesus with the people there. Now, for a white man to be in a black barroom in the Mississippi Delta was pretty crazy. I was as out of place as a milk bucket under a bull. But God had sent me there. I was misunderstood and even threatened with knives. But I also saw people kneel openly on those streets to receive Jesus Christ as their Lord and Savior. One man told me that he would cut me up. I remembered what David Wilkerson had said under similar circumstances and told the man, "You can cut me up, but Jesus still loves you, and so do I." He just couldn't believe that God had really sent me there, and that was my motivation.

I went in and out of bars and beer joints sharing Jesus for several years until the Lord led me into different ministry. I had experienced several dangerous situations, but the Lord always delivered me out of each of them and spread the fragrance of His presence to the people there. I grew to feel fairly comfortable sharing the gospel in such places.

But when I got older, had children, and was put in different situations, somehow things begin to change. In later life we often have to deal with fears and worries that we didn't have to deal with before. As Pastor Mike Mille puts it, "Higher level, bigger devil." Or at least, different devils. That is true, and so, if we are to grow and take our Promised Land, we'll have to deal with different temptations and spiritual attacks as well. The Lord may also allow our faith to be tested or call us to do something that requires more faith stretching than we have had to do before. As Spurgeon said, "Fair weather faith is no faith at all."

In this book, I describe how, at a point in my Christian life and ministry, I was surprised by attacks of fear and panic that seemed to come out of nowhere. Some of these attacks that I describe were various alarming fears and worries that occurred in different circumstances and situations. I was not accustomed to feeling fears and worry that much, so these experiences took me by surprise. They were beginning to influence the way I thought and acted. So I began to seek God earnestly. As I was forced to deal with these attacks, I knew that what I was experiencing was not the way the Lord intended life to be! Through seeking the Lord and studying His Word, the Holy Spirit reminded me of teachings, and revealed to me principles, meditations and strategies that set me free. "You will know the truth, and the truth will make you free" (**John 8:32**).

Paul said that he would glory in his weakness because God's power was perfected in weakness (**2 Cor. 12:9**). I shared with friends and family, and also in Sunday messages, my weaknesses and struggles, and the things the Lord was showing me to help me overcome. Some of the listeners told me of their battles with fear. I found out that many were experiencing the exact same fears that had attacked and tormented me. They said that I should put these teachings in book form to help more people. I also heard other "big name" pastors and church leaders tell of their struggles with fear. I realized that this wasn't just a problem that I was dealing with. Not only average church members, but also many church leaders and pastors were struggling with fears and worry too. I sensed the Holy Spirit confirming in my spirit that it truly was God's will for me to share my experiences and testimony. The result is this book.

God wants His people to be free from tormenting spirits of fear, worry and panic. The body of Christ is, by in large, not ready for what is coming upon the world, be it calamity or world harvest. We are not ready for the things that 'cause men's heart to fail them." In fact, in many cases, a great number Christians think that Jesus is returning to rescue us out of all these problems that are increasing in the world. But one thing is for sure. We aren't going to be ready to face the difficult times that come upon us if we are plagued and bound by fear and worry. Things aren't getting easier. They are getting worse with each passing year. We also won't be able to reach the world for Jesus Christ and take the

Gospel to the ends of the earth if we don't learn to be the overcomers that we are called to be.

My desire is that you will overcome, walk in freedom, and know how to use the spiritual weapons God has given you to defeat any demon of fear that tries to stop you from fulfilling God's will for your life. God wants us to win any battle against dread and panic in our lives. If you put to practice the truths and strategies I have highlighted in this book, there is no doubt that you will experience greater freedom from fear and worry. You'll begin to enjoy the peace of God that passes all understanding, even in the midst of storms and battles. This is what we need in order to reap a mighty harvest in the days ahead. Let's do it!

Clay Brooks

1

DREAMS AND NIGHTMARES

"In a dream, a vision of the night,
When sound sleep falls on men, While they
slumber in their beds."—**Job 33:15**

Gunshots went off not far from the remote, rustic, Chinese hotel where we were staying. Immediately we were wondering what was going on. It was April 2006, and my co-worker Mike Robertson and I were in the mountainous, forest-filled Baima (bye-mah) territory of northern Sichuan Province, China. The Baima people are one of the approximately 500 different ethnic people groups in China. We went there because research indicated that 0% of the Baima people had heard the gospel, and therefore there was not a single Christian among them. God had put a call in our hearts to find these people and reach them with the good news of Jesus Christ.

Early that morning we had headed north from the Provincial capital, Chengdu, for about six or seven hours through lush, green mountains and valleys. It is home to monkeys, pandas, rare birds, and even old, overgrown, WWII Flying Tiger airfields. It is also the area in China known for the tragic, 7.9 earthquake that happened in 2008 in which an estimated 86,000 people were killed.

We asked the other two or three guests in the hotel what was going on with the gunshots. They told us that people were shooting their guns to scare demons away. Whenever the Chinese have a wedding, open a new business, move into a new apartment, or celebrate the beginning of the Chinese New Year, they shoot fireworks. But in the case of the Baima, they don't mess around. They use guns! They wanted to *really* get rid of those demons!

To most Chinese people today it's probably just a way of celebrating the event, and they don't really know why they shoot fireworks. But it actually does come from the ancient superstition that the noise would help scare away any demons that might be lurking around, wanting to spoil the event. Well, I thought, praise God, I don't have to have a gun to get rid of demons. The name of Jesus will put any demon to flight.

As we went to bed that night, I read some Bible verses, meditated on them and went on to sleep. I try to put God's thoughts in my mind before I go to bed so the devil won't have any room to insert his twisted thoughts and dreams. During the night, I had a very profound dream from the Lord. It was a very significant dream for me. For months, and even years, before this, I had been tormented off and on by different panic and fear attacks from the devil. They were designed by him to try to hinder me from going out to preach the gospel among unreached people groups in remote places. And the dream confirmed to me the way to freedom, which the Lord had actually revealed to me not long before this trip. But before I continue, let me explain just a little about dreams.

One of the ways God spoke to His people in the Bible was through dreams. He even led Joseph, the guardian father of His Son Jesus, by dreams instead of by some other way that we might think would have been more logical or reasonable. And since the Bible says that God hasn't changed (**Hebrews 13:8**), we can expect Him to sometimes speak to us this way also. In fact, I've found in China that God often speaks to illiterate Christians through dreams. They certainly can't read the Bible for themselves in order to hear God. I've also read many testimonies of Muslims who had Jesus appear to them in a dream and speak to them, convincing them that He was the truth. The Lord even revealed a very important principle and truth to Peter through a trance (**Acts 10:10**)!

Some Christians today would think that it's weird if they heard someone say that they had a dream from God or went into a trance. That's because they are led more by their lack of personal experience than the teachings of the Bible, and the experiences of Bible characters. And since they themselves haven't experienced such a trance or dream, they think that anyone who has is suspect, at best, or maybe of the devil, at worst! But God often uses the seemingly foolish things such as visions, dreams, and trances to test us, as well as sometimes even offend and confound our pride or know-it-all attitude.

Of course, we all know the weirdos whose made-up dreams or interpretations turn us all off. And also God tells us to test spiritual revelations (**1 John 4:1**), and that we should accept no dream or vision that is contrary to the Bible. And yet, God still chooses to use such ways as these to guide us, and also test our hearts even today. And so with this very short introduction on dreams, let's get back to the story.

Before this experience in the Baima area, I hadn't had that many dreams from the Lord. So I was somewhat surprised by this dream. And the dream seemed to be very significant too. Plus I remembered it, which normally I didn't.

Now in the dream, I was in the house where I grew up as a child. A terrorist had burst in to do what they do, and as he moved in further, I confronted him. I was trying to get my gloves off so I could use the gun I had in my hands. I wanted to shoot him. The gloves were hindering me. I could tell that he was the leader and that more were outside. Finally, in a desperate attempt, I got the gloves off, raised my gun, and then shot and killed him. I was heading toward the door to deal with the others when I woke up.

As I woke up I knew exactly what the meaning of the dream was. God was confirming to me what I needed to keep doing in order to maintain the freedom I had recently gained against tormenting, terroristic thoughts and fears that had plagued me off and on for several years.

In the dream, the gun in my hand represented, not only the Bible (the Word of God), but also my understanding of how to use it. It is one of our spiritual weapons (**Ephesians 6:17**). But unless one is trained to know how to use it, it is not of much use against the devil and his attacks. The man-made gun that I had heard before I went to sleep that night was useless in scaring any demons or fear away. But the weapon of the Word of God is very powerful against demonic terrorist attacks.

Jesus used the Word of God when He resisted the devil in the wilderness. In the end of that encounter with the tempter, Jesus also used authority to command Satan to leave (**Matthew 4:10**). Jesus has told us that we too, as His disciples and body, can and should do the same things that He did (**John 14:12**). He has given us authority to use His Word and His name in resisting the devil, fear, and whatever evil comes against us (**James 4:7; Mark 16:17; Ephesians 6:11, 13; 1 Peter 5:8, 9**). But in order for these weapons to be effective, we have to use them. He's not going to do it for us. In the dream, ***I*** had to shoot the gun. This is a very important point! Don't miss it.

A gun has bullets, or at least, it should have bullets. If not, it is useless. To be effective, to accomplish what a gun was created for, you have to load the bullets into the gun, and then shoot the bullets. Metaphorically speaking, bullets are like individual Scriptures and passages in the Bible. They are ammunition that can help us in spiritual battles. They can destroy evil, terroristic thoughts. Of course, they bring strength, comfort, and refreshing, but they are also weapons in our arsenal. We must learn to load our spiritual weapon and then pull the trigger at the terrorist thoughts that attack us.

How do you load your weapon? You find Scriptures that help you in your situation. Then you meditate on those verses until they get into your spirit, and you believe them. You memorize, pray over, sing, and quote those Scriptures that help you with whatever fear or worry you are dealing with.

In my case, it was different fears that were plaguing me off and on. My point here that I want you to get is that I needed to take the time to meditate on (not just read) the Word of God. I needed to load my spiritual gun and then use it. I needed to memorize, and review over and over certain Scriptures, or my spiritual gun would have been empty, at least as far as helping me against those fears was concerned. If I didn't take the time to load it properly, when I raised it up there would only have been the empty click, click, click sound of an empty gun.

By meditating, reviewing, and memorizing the verses that helped me to resist the devil and fear, I was loading my gun, my spiritual weapon. Too many Christians either have an empty gun or one with very few bullets. And we have to learn that just like regular guns, spiritual guns have to not just be loaded to be useful, but be reloaded as well. And the trigger must be pulled. It must be fired to be effective.

How do we pull the trigger and fire our spiritual weapon? We pull the trigger and fire by releasing our faith in God's Word through prayer, as well as confessing and declaring it with our mouths. You can have the Word in you, but not utilize it if you don't believe it, pray it, and then also confess and declare it in your life. Pulling the trigger also means to take action. Faith without works is dead, the Bible tells us. We have to go forward, face our fears and defeat them, in Jesus' name!

Before this dream, off and on for several years, I had been having demonic attacks of fear come out of nowhere against my mind. They were sometimes like panic attacks that would come in different situations. It was affecting my sleep at times, and also hindering me from doing certain ministry activities that I knew God wanted me to do. I would have to quote Scripture, rebuke fear, and fervently cry out to God when I would unexpectedly find myself coming under attacks of fear and anxiety. And although after a while I would find temporary relief, I couldn't find a way to permanently stop the fear attacks from coming.

As you can imagine, I had sought the Lord diligently as to why this was happening and how to gain victory over these tormenting experiences. I knew that that kind of mental torment was not from God, nor was it God's will. Now, here in Baima territory, the Lord was confirming to me through the dream how to stay free. The reason the Lord gave me the dream on this trip is because it was often on trips like this that I would be attacked with fearful thoughts that would try to rob me of sleep and peace.

The devil didn't want me to go on such ministry outreaches in the first place. I normally didn't have such attacks if I stayed at home. So the Lord was revealing to me that the answer to my deliverance lay in using the sword/gun of the Spirit, the Word of God.

But I *was* already spending time in the Word of God every day, as well as preparing messages every week to share on Sundays. Why wasn't that enough? Well, what was becoming more evident was that the devil had put a demonic '*hit job*' out on me. There were demonic assassins assigned to take me out of action. Not to literally kill me, but to stop me from going out and preaching the gospel to others. I was getting hit with strategic, demonic ambushes, not just a general fear that we all might experience in the world at times. Getting the revelation about these assassins attacking me was giving me truth, light, and helping to set me free.

The other action I needed to do was to use the Word of God in a more specific, concentrated, and lethal way against the specific terroristic, demonic thoughts that were tormenting me. Of course, I already knew this would help. But what I didn't fully realize was how much more specific and concentrated action I needed to take. Sometimes just one bullet won't take out a terrorist. Sometimes you even need a bomb to blow him out of a bunker!

I still needed to keep general reading and meditating on God's Word, but even more so I needed to reload my spiritual gun with a higher caliber of spiritual bullets. I needed to use specific bullets designed to take out the specific terrorists coming against the peace of God in my mind and spirit. Those terroristic, fearful thoughts were trying to hold me hostage. Putting it another way, I needed to take a more correctly prescribed medicine (specific Scriptures), as well as a greater dose of His Word-medicine designed for my personal problems.

One of the reasons many Christians are experiencing more problems with fear and worry is the increase of danger and uncertainty in the times in which we are living. But also there is another reason. Sometimes we have not built the foundation of our lives on the rock of *doing* God's Word (being a *doer* of the Word) like Jesus said we should (**Matthew 7:24-28**). We should have grown more spiritually but we haven't. We should already be *doers* of the Word. There are things in the Word of God that we are told to do with worry and fear. If we don't do it, then we'll suffer for it.

So we should be meditating more in the Word of God, but many times we aren't. And therefore, with our defenses down, or at least not as strong as they should be, we find ourselves getting hit in bigger battles and attacks that come against us. More arrows of the enemy find ways to get through our defenses and hit us.

At times God also allows the attacks in order to teach us, train us, cause us to seek Him more, and help our faith to grow. If we stay at the same place where we've been spiritually, we aren't growing and won't be able to stand against or defeat the increasing demonic attacks coming against our peace. We won't be able to deal with the increasing levels of demonic fear that are growing in the world as we get closer and closer to the return of Jesus.

Now the main reason the devil was attacking me is that I was on the offensive, taking the gospel into unreached areas, probing into enemy territory, threatening his hold on what he felt were long-secure areas of his domain. He didn't want unreached people to hear about Jesus. Often the devil won't bother us if we don't bother him. If we just stay back in our easy chair behind secure lines, our comfort zones, and don't cross over into enemy lines, he'll leave us alone, at least for a while. So one of the reasons you might not be dealing with any kind of fear in your life is that you aren't trying to take any new territory for God. You aren't reaching out to the lost, confronting sin in society, or taking the good news to those who have never heard of Jesus.

But many of you who are reading this now are involved in spreading the kingdom of God. You are seeking to please the Lord in all you do. You are actively sharing your faith and therefore a threat to the devil and his kingdom. And as a result, you too may be dealing with different kinds of demonic attacks of fear and worry. You may even be like I was, on a demonic assassin's hit list, and find yourself ambushed by fear and worry designed to take you out of action and stop you from fulfilling your divine destiny.

Whatever the case may be, Jesus has given us powerful spiritual weapons not only to *get* free from fear and worry, but also to *stay* free. Thank God we don't have to stay in bondage to tormenting thoughts and panic attacks. Jesus came to set the captives free! Hallelujah!

2

THE FOUNDATION FOR PEACE

What Lies At The Bottom Of The Ocean
And Twitches? A Nervous Wreck.

Ignorance breeds fear. It is very important to understand this. Put another way, fear grows in a culture of ignorance. **Amos 4:6** says, "My people are destroyed for lack of knowledge." We have to know what God's Word says in relation to fear and worry, or any subject for that matter, in order to live as God wants us to live. Likewise, we must know that Jesus not only defeated death and hell, but He also overcame fear and worry when He died and rose from the grave. We have to get to know our Heavenly Father God, and His Son Jesus, the Prince of Peace intimately. Having a good relationship with our earthly father helps us to know Him and trust Him completely. Getting to know our Heavenly Father through His Word, through promises in the Bible, through experiences in life, and through prayer also help us learn to trust Him as well.

Not long before the experience I had with the dream (in chapter one), I read Dodie Osteen's book "*Healed of Cancer*" for the second time. Actually, many years ago at Bethany World Prayer Center, in Baton Rouge, LA, I had personally heard Sister Osteen and Pastor John together share her testimony of how she was healed of terminal cancer of the liver. The doctors only gave her a couple of months to live. Her own son, who is a doctor, wept when he heard the diagnosis because he knew that she, under normal circumstances, had no chance to live. But she didn't just simply accept the death sentence she had heard, the way many Christians would do today. She knew that God also had something to say about the situation. She made a list of about 40 Scriptures concerning healing from the Bible. She would meditate on those verses every day. She would speak them forth. She saturated her mind and spirit with the truth of healing in God's Word.

Then she acted like God's Word was true, even though in her body she didn't feel that way at all. In reality, she felt very weak and very ill. But she still persevered and kept on living until a year later when the doctors declared her completely free of cancer. Even to this day she will not leave her house until she has meditated on those same verses on healing. When she passes a graveyard, she shouts out loud, "I will live and not die and declare the works of the Lord!" The point I am getting to here is that her strategy for healing will also work for bringing peace and deliverance from fearful thoughts.

Notice that she began to spend much more time meditating on the Word of God that pertained to her specific situation. It became like her spiritual medicine from her Heavenly Physician, which, in fact, the Word of God is. **Proverbs 4:20-23** says this about God's Word.

> "My son, give attention to my words;
> Incline your ear to my sayings.
> Do not let them depart from your sight;
> Keep them in the midst of your heart.
> For they are life to those who find them,
> And health to all their body.
> Watch over your heart with all diligence,
> For from it flow the springs of life."
> (My underlining added.)

The reason most of us don't have the results in life that we want is that, in many cases, we aren't willing to give this much attention to God's Word. But this is precisely the reason why we don't have the results sometimes that God's Word promises us. When the doctor gives us the prescription we have to follow his directions if we want the results. We must do the same with God, Jehovah-Rapha, the Lord our Healer. We must give Him the same amount of confidence and respect, even more, than we would give an earthly doctor. Sometimes we have to take medicine for several days before we begin to see and feel the results. We need to do the same thing with God and His Word. The fact of the matter is that many times we just really don't believe God and His Word the way we think we do. The scary thing is that we do this without realizing it. And then, the way we act and think about it reveals that we think God's Word just really doesn't work.

Hebrews 2:1 also affirms this truth of needing to spend more time in the Word of God in order to get results.

> "For this reason we must pay much closer attention to what we have heard, so that we

> do not drift away from it." (My underlining emphasis added.)

Our tendency is to drift away from the truths and promises of the Word. Only by "*paying much closer attention*" can we hope to stay anchored to the solid rock of God's Word, and get the promised results.

Truth is of utmost importance in order to establish God's kingdom in our lives. It is a vital part of the very foundation on which we build and enjoy all the other blessings of God. And **Psalm 51:6** says, "Behold, You desire truth in the innermost being," the deepest part of our being, the spirit and thoughts of man. If we want to be free and experience all the victory that God has won for us through Jesus, we must believe God's truth about life, about ourselves, and the experiences that we are going through. If we knowingly or unknowingly have negative influences or anything not based on truth in our innermost beliefs, then that doubt or lie will affect us spiritually, and in all our experiences in life.

The devil wants doubt, lies, and fears in our innermost being. He is a "liar and the father of lies" (**John 8:44**). We must agree with God's truth and desire it in our innermost being. Desiring truth and being willing to admit when we believe wrong things is critical in winning our spiritual battles. Any army that believes the enemy's lies and propaganda will be defeated and enslaved. When we believe truth and have it settled in our innermost being, then God's kingdom will be established in our lives, and the devil and darkness will be kicked out!

After I read Dodie Osteen's book the second time, the Holy Spirit spoke to me that what she had done held a key part for me also winning the war against the fear attacks that I was dealing with. So I put together a list of about 20 Scriptures that ministered peace, faith, confidence, and security to me. I began to meditate on those Scriptures every day, without fail. I didn't meditate on them just once a day. I did it when I got up and also before I went to bed, as well as during the day. As I began to do this I found that the attacks of fear, dread and worry began to melt away, and then, not long after this, I had the dream I told you about in chapter one.

Before this I had commanded fear to leave and resisted it, but even though I knew I had authority over fear, it wasn't working for me. Why? Because my spiritual weapon, my faith gun wasn't fully loaded. So even though we know we have authority over fear in Jesus' name, if our authority is not thoroughly based and loaded with faith-building Scriptures, it won't work. Our spiritual weapon, our faith gun is not properly loaded and won't fire. After the dream I knew that God was showing me that I needed to meditate on those specific Scriptures, and then my faith would be loaded! With a loaded faith, terrorizing thoughts and spirits of fear now ran from me! And praise God, I was totally set free and could sleep with peace and calm, "free from the dread of evil" (**Prov. 1:33**).

As I began to meditate more on the Word of God, I found out that I didn't have to command the fear to leave. It was just gone! I'm not saying that sometimes we don't have to command it to leave. I'm just saying that sometimes commanding is not what is needed as much as simple meditating and feeding on the truth of God's Word.

Meditating on the Word of God might be something new to you. Maybe you just read or study the Word. **Psalm 19:14** says, "Let the words of my mouth and the **meditation** of my heart be acceptable in your sight, O Lord, my rock and my redeemer."

Meditating is to ponder, think about and consider something over and over. In Hebrew (The language of the Old Testament) it comes from the idea of a cow chewing the cud. It swallows the grass and then brings it back up and chews it over again. When we do this with the Word of God, it begins to get more deeply into our spirit, our heart. And it is in the heart where faith is born. The fact of the matter is that many times we are already meditating or pondering things, but we didn't realize it. And the problem is we are meditating on worry and fear! God wants the meditations of our heart to be acceptable to Him. In order to be acceptable, they must be filled with faith and truth from His Word.

I heard Reverend Kenneth Hagin Sr. share one time about an experience he had in 1944 when he was delivered from the fear of being paralyzed again. He had gone through a time when he was almost totally paralyzed for about a year, and doctors said that he was going to die. Then when he was sixteen years of age, he was supernaturally healed of the paralysis by faith in the Word of God found in Mark 11:23, 24. But the trauma of being paralyzed had opened the door for a spirit of fear to torment him off and on for the next ten years after the healing. The devil would tell him that the paralysis was going to return. Bro. Hagin said, "That fear had followed me like a little dog for ten years, ever since I had been miraculously healed as a teenage boy. It sat by my bed every night. But one night in bed, as I read *Healing From Heaven* by Dr. Lilian B. Yeomans, I received the revelation that Satan was the author of all sickness and fear. I looked around, and that fear was gone! I didn't even have to tell it to leave. I just found out the truth, and the truth set me free!" He said, "I got so thrilled, I turned on the light, jumped out of bed, and ran around the room! I couldn't stay in bed --- I was just so thrilled with the Word!" You can see that his experience is similar to Sister Osteen's in that when meditating either on the truth of God's Word, in the Bible itself, or on a teaching in written form based on that truth, the result was peace, freedom, and deliverance.

Fear, worry, and dread are all manifestations of wrong thoughts. Many times these thoughts are instigated by demons, spirits of fear. **2 Timothy 1:7** tells us that "God hasn't given us a spirit of fear (or timidity), but of power, love, and a sound mind." A sound mind is a peaceful mind. It is a mind that meditates and thinks on God's truths. **Philippians 4:6-8** tells us what to do with worried thoughts. It also tells us the right things to meditate on.

> "Be anxious for nothing, but in everything by prayer and supplication with thanksgiving let your requests be made known to God.
> And the peace of God, which surpasses all comprehension, will guard your hearts and your minds in Christ Jesus.
> Finally, brethren, whatever is true, whatever is honorable, whatever is right, whatever is pure, whatever is lovely, whatever is of good repute, if there is any excellence and if anything worthy of praise, dwell on these things."
> (My underlining emphasis added.)

Actually we are commanded here in these verses to not worry or be anxious about anything. So how do we obey this in practical terms? First, we pray and ask God to work in the situation that worries us. Then we thank Him for hearing our prayer and answering us. We do this even though we haven't seen the manifestation of the answer yet with our eyes. That is putting our faith into action. Then, and only then, will His supernatural peace begin to guard our heart and mind.

Next, in order to *keep* the peace, enforce the peace like a policeman (a peace officer), we must do what verse eight says. We must dwell on these positive kinds of thoughts, which agree with God's Word. These kinds of thoughts are the only thing that will help us to maintain peace and joy in our hearts. It won't just happen by itself. You have to actively pursue meditating on these things, just like what someone in pain would do by taking medicine in order to stop it. If they didn't know how to receive healing from God, they would faithfully and religiously take their medicine.

Many times it's simply a matter of how badly you want something spiritually. Jacob, the second born son of Isaac, intensely wanted the birthright and the blessing that was normally intended for the first born son in a family. Esau, the firstborn son, was cavalier and careless about God's blessings, and the Bible says this showed that he actually "*despised*" the spiritual blessings of God (**Genesis 25:34**). Jacob didn't always use the right methods, but he hungered and thirsted for God's spiritual blessings, and we must do the same. We must show that we put first priority and importance on God and His Word. When we honor God in this way, He says that He will honor us, reward us and bless us. Of course, sometimes we just haven't been taught these things. But when we have been taught, or have seen the truth for ourselves, God will then begin to expect us to obey His Word, and grow into strong, mature believers so that we can live in victory, and begin to help others also.

Of course, the foundation of peace in our lives begins when you believe in and receive Jesus Christ as your Lord, Master, and Savior. He is the Prince of Peace. When you are born again, you receive the only true foundation of peace in life, Jesus Christ Himself, living inside you. If you haven't done so, or if there is any doubt in your heart concerning Jesus being your Lord and Savior, make that decision today. Repent of your sins. Ask God to forgive you. Proclaim Jesus as your Master and Savior. Then you'll have true peace with God.

Scripture list

Here is the list of Scriptures, and more, that I meditated on to get free from the fears and worries that were plaguing me. Look these up. Meditate on them and find the ones that help you the most. Memorize them and hide them in your heart, and they will begin to bring peace to your life. The truth will set you free.

Psalm 1:1-3, Genesis 28:15 & Deuteronomy 28:6, Exodus 23:20 & Matthew 18:10, Psalm 23, Psalm 27:1-3, 10, Psalm 34:4, 7-10, Psalm 37:25 & Isaiah 46:3,4, Psalm 46:1-3, Psalm 62:6 & Isaiah 54:10, Psalm 91, Colossians 3:15, Psalm 118:6, Romans 8:6, Psalm 121:7, 8, Proverbs 12:25 & Psalm 56:3, 4, Proverbs 1:33, Proverbs 3:13, 17, 24-26, Jeremiah 29:11 & Psalm 138:8, Isaiah 41:10, Isaiah 26:3, John 14:27, Matthew 6:11, 25-34, Hebrews 13:5, 6, Luke 8:50, John 14:1, 2 Corinthians 10:4, 5 & 2 Timothy 1:7, Psalm 139:23 & Psalm 4:8, 1 Peter 5:6, 7, Philippians 4:6-9, John 14:1, 27, John 16:33 & Psalm 50:15

3

GOD'S SLEEPING PILL

"Dad, I'm gonna sleep well tonight."
(Isaac, my six yr. old son)
"Why, son?"
"Because all my worries are gone."

They had threatened to fine me heavily, and or put me in jail for two weeks! In March 2007, somehow we had overlooked our two sons visa expiration date, and the Chinese customs authorities weren't happy about it. We had gone almost two months over their expiration date before we realized it. Now we were in big trouble. I thought they would be understanding and glad that we had come and brought the problem to their attention. But they didn't see it that way.

When they told me I might have to spend two weeks in jail, I have to admit, I began to get concerned. Worry and fear began to crawl over me like a cold, slithery boa constrictor. They told me they'd let me know in a few days what they decided. I told my wife, co-workers and friends in China, and we began to pray.

What I didn't tell my wife is that the police amazingly asked me, "How busy are you? Maybe your wife could come in and take your place? She could spend the two weeks in jail." Well, I'm not stupid. I didn't tell my wife about that until after the whole problem had been resolved.

The first couple of days, I struggled with fear and worry. I didn't much like the prospect of spending two weeks in a Chinese jail. Of course, that's not anything compared with the amount of time some of my Chinese brothers and sisters were spending in jail. But still it began to affect my sleep. I couldn't get to sleep. My mind was racing. We let our home church, as well as several other churches and friends back in the States, know what was happening, and they were praying for us. I wrote to my pastor, and a few other pastor friends about my situation and asked them to pray. Their support and encouraging words were what helped put me over, and give me the victory. My pastor, Rod Aguillard wrote, "*Got your back covered! It is all working for your good. If God be for you, who can be against you*?" Just those three short sentences brought peace and calm to my spirit. Also knowing that I wasn't alone, and people were praying for us was just the support I needed. After that, I was able to rest peacefully and had no trouble getting to sleep.

The Chinese authorities assumed that I was afraid and might try to leave town or fly out of the country. So they stationed a plainclothes policeman in a hooded jacket to watch outside our apartment. Early one morning I took our puppy Toby out to go to the bathroom. As we ran out, he went right by the agent staked out in front of our building. He had his back turned to us in the darkness. As we ran past him, he whirled around in surprise. Startled, he quickly left as we ran around the corner. From then on I think they knew I wasn't going to try to bolt and flee.

The Chinese authorities ended up giving me the smallest fine possible, and not making me spend any time at all in jail. Praise God. And thank God for the body of Christ! Thank God for the Word of God and encouraging words from His body, the church.

Let me ask you a question. Please imagine and consider this carefully. How would you feel if you were threatened with jail time for your faith in Jesus? Maybe some of you have already spent time in jail for your faith. But most Christians in the West have not. How would you handle it if you knew that because of your stand for traditional marriage, or some other Bible truth, you were threatened with jail? What if the government told you not to preach certain parts of the Bible or they would take away your tax-exempt status and put you in jail? It's one thing to say, "I would still preach and stand for truth." But it's another thing when jail time is actually staring you in the face.

The Bible says in **2 Timothy 3:12**, "Indeed, all who desire to live godly in Christ Jesus will be persecuted." Have you prepared your heart, mind and emotions for the possibility of jail, prison or even death, because of your stand for the Lord? Jesus told us that persecution was coming and that if they hated Him, they would hate us (**Mt. 10:22; John 18:15**). Paul stated it very plainly in this verse. If we truly seek to live a godly life, we will be persecuted. Period. It may take different forms and shapes in different countries and situations, but the fact of the matter is that every Christian should know and expect to be persecuted.

And I'm not talking about Christians being obnoxious and hateful. What was hateful about Jesus? He was pure love, but also pure righteousness. And He was crucified for it. We must wake up. We must slap ourselves out of our sleep and realize that we are in a serious spiritual battle. Persecution is no longer just over in Africa, Asia, Cuba, or some place other than where we live in the West. Jesus told us many times to "watch and pray." You have been misled if you think it's normal for you to not be mistreated as a Christian. That is abnormal.

Most Christians aren't living the kind of moral, godly life that Jesus is talking about. If you take a stand for moral purity, man and woman marriage, and the hot-button moral issues of your day, then you will be hated. If you affirm that homosexuality is a sin and that abortion is not only the killing, but also the murder of an unborn child, you will be marked. If you speak out about these things and if you share your faith in the workplace and out in life, you will take heat. If you do sidewalk counseling, minister or protest in front of an abortion/baby-killing center, you will take abuse, be hated, and persecuted. Darkness hates the light, my friends.

But if you never speak out, never witness to others of your faith in Jesus, and instead just stay at home in your easy chair, not living a godly, moral life, then you won't be persecuted. You see, true godliness requires action. God is not a coward. He not only speaks the truth in love, but He also takes righteous action. Jesus was hated because of the things that He said and did, not for sitting at home in his easy chair! It might seem much easier to get a good night's sleep when you don't seek to live a truly godly life, than to take a stand for righteousness, truth, and justice. Initially you don't receive the threats or take much heat. Why? Because you don't rock the boat. But sooner or later, if you really love God, your conscience will begin to bother you because you aren't living the way you should. You aren't taking a stand for Christ. You aren't sharing your faith.

Pastor Moses Xie of China, who spent 23 years in prison for his faith, told us of how he struggled when he was first arrested back in May of 1956. He was tortured. They wanted him to join the Communist Three-self Church of China. He refused. He tearfully admitted how at one point he even tried to kill himself. But finally, he said that he heard the voice of the Lord quote to him **2 Corinthians 12:9**, "My grace is sufficient for you." And with that encouragement and grace, he was able to lift up his head and walk with the Lord through 23 years in the Chinese Laogai, which is the name of Communist China's "reform through labor" prison system.

Why am I sharing his testimony? There is a lesson to be learned. God's grace is sufficient, but we need to prepare. We need to seriously consider before the Lord how we would respond to the prospect of jail time or prison for our faith. Only then will we be ready to face the storms and trials that are upon us. Jesus warned us.

You may be thinking that something like that would never happen to you or in your country. Don't be a fool. Wake up. Read the writing on the wall. Get prepared to not only survive through whatever persecution may come your way, but even more to overcome and share your faith boldly whether in freedom or in bondage. Start by visiting those in prison. Share the gospel with them. Jesus told us to. Then, at least you'll have gotten used to the feel of a jailhouse. And maybe you'll already have some friends in there to greet you if you are ever sent there. That's a thought.

Daniel found himself in much, much hotter water than I was in my opening story back at the beginning of this chapter. Remember the story of Daniel in the lion's den (**Daniel 6**)? He was framed in a political ploy by the satraps, prefects and politicians of his day to try to take him out and get his position in the government. They formed a cabal but couldn't find any wrongdoing, corruption, or immorality in Daniel's life through which they would be able to accuse him and remove him from his powerful position before the king. So they devised a way to set in place laws that would incriminate Daniel because of his pure devotion to God. They said if anyone prays to anybody else besides the king, or to any other God, for 30 days, he should be thrown into the lion's den. When Daniel knew the king had signed the law, he went straight to his room and proceeded to pray as he had always done. As a result, he was arrested, and the king had no choice but to throw him into the lion's den. Let's pick up the story where it continues in Daniel chapter six.

> 18 Then the king went off to his palace and spent the night fasting, and no entertainment was brought before him; and his sleep fled from him.
>
> 19 Then the king arose at dawn, at the break of day, and went in haste to the lions' den.
>
> 20 When he had come near the den to Daniel, he cried out with a troubled voice. The king spoke and said to Daniel, "Daniel, servant of the living God, has your God, whom you constantly serve, been able to deliver you from the lions?"
>
> 21 Then Daniel spoke to the king, "O king, live forever!
>
> 22 "My God sent His angel and shut the lions' mouths and they have not harmed me, inasmuch as I was found innocent before Him;

> and also toward you, O king, I have committed no crime." (**Daniel 6:18-22**)

Notice the king, in verse 18, who appreciated Daniel and was going to place him over his entire kingdom, couldn't sleep all night. He was worried about Daniel. But I'm sure that Daniel, on the other hand, knowing the Lord's angel was there beside him shutting the mouths of the lions, slept like a baby all night long. Sooner or later, I guess the lions got frustrated, gave up, and went on to sleep too. So we could say that Daniel slept with the lions that night. Praise God, He can shut the mouths of doubt, fear, and worry that try to keep us awake all night.

The Bible also says that Daniel was "*innocent before*" the Lord. Having a clear conscience is certainly another one of the keys to having a good night's sleep. Daniel knew the Lord was with him. God's angels are round about you protecting you. If you also have a clear conscience "before the Lord" that makes for a great foundation for sweet sleep even in the most terrifying of circumstances in life.

You may think, "Well, that was great for Daniel. He had an angel there with him, shutting the lion's mouths." Thankfully, the fact is that WE DO TOO! Look at **Psalm 34:7**. "The angel of the LORD encamps around those who fear Him, and rescues them." **Psalm 91:11, 12** also tell us, "For He will give His angels charge concerning you, To guard you in all your ways. They will bear you up in their hands, that you do not strike your foot against a stone." We just need to make sure that we have confessed and repented of our sins. Then we need to believe that He has forgiven us and cleansed us (**1 John 1:9**) and made us innocent by the blood of Jesus. Of course, we need to dwell and live close to God (**Psalm 91:1**). That's exactly what Daniel was doing. So we can claim the same kind of protection that Daniel had. You may think, "But I'm not Daniel." But you are a child of God. And Daniel didn't have the blood of Jesus available to him like we do now. God is even more eager to forgive and demonstrate His love and protection toward us through the sacrifice of His Son.

Now all those crooked politicians probably slept well that night, but it was to be their last night of sleep on earth. And they haven't slept a wink since that night because they were thrown into the lion's den in place of Daniel, and have been in eternal punishment ever since. Sin has wages that it pays, and a good night's sleep is not part of it. It caught up with them in the end. The Bible says, "God is not mocked; for whatever a man sows, this he will also reap" (**Galatians 6:7**).

At the beginning of this chapter, I have a quote from my youngest son when he was six years old. Evidently he had heard either myself or someone else teach or preach on God wanting to take all our cares and worries. We were getting ready for bed when he told me, "*Dad, I'm gonna sleep well tonight.*" I smiled at such an adult statement coming from a six-year-old and questioned, "*Why, Isaac*?" He answered, "*Because all my worries are gone.*" I had a good laugh, but what he said was absolutely true. I really think that God was using him to speak to me about the very truth we're talking about here, but I didn't catch it at the time. Thankfully, he didn't have too much that might tempt him to worry. He might have had some problems with bad dreams or being afraid of the dark a few times, but not much more than that. Of course, if our parents were fearful and worrying people, we might have picked up worry habits from them. In the first place, adults also have more situations in life the devil can use to tempt them to worry. The point is that worries can inhibit our sleep and make it hard to get to sleep. In fact, this is what was happening to me that I wrote about at the beginning of the book. When fear and worry begin to grow in our lives, one of the first areas that will be affected is our sleep. But, praise God, He hasn't left us to fend for ourselves. We can be free to sleep like the proverbial baby, without a care or worry in the world. In fact, that is precisely God's will for every single one of us. But in this fallen world, our sleep isn't always a given fact that we can take for granted. Many times we'll have to "fight the good fight of faith" to get a good night's sleep. (**1 Tim.6:12**)

Of course, sleep is a vital and important part of our daily lives. We were created to sleep each day, and therefore we spend a large portion of every twenty-four hour period in sleep. At least that is the way that God intended it to be. For a lot of people, that is wishful thinking though because they don't sleep very well, at all. Someone has said, "*Money can buy medicine, but not health; a bed, but not sleep*." We need adequate sleep and rest to get rejuvenated every day. This is the way God created and designed us. In fact, God Himself is our example concerning rest. The Bible says that even God rested on the seventh day and commanded us to rest also. So rest and sleep is something very important to God. He Himself doesn't sleep but has given us sleep as a blessing. Look at what **Psalm 127** says about how God gives to us, His "beloved", sleep.

> It is vain for you to rise up early,
> To sit up late,
> To eat the bread of sorrows;
> For so He [God] gives His beloved sleep.
> —**Psalm 127:2**

A contemporary version of the first part of this Psalm, the negative part, might read like James Thurber's *Fables for Our Times*, 1940 (Although I did change one word.).

> **Early to rise and *late* to bed**
> **Makes a man healthy and wealthy and dead.**

All the rushing, hustling and bustling that modern man does to try to get ahead really only give rise to a much lower level of life, creativity, and joy. Like one minister said, "The Lord told me that if I keep going as I'm going I might win the rat race, but I'd still be a rat." And so for different reasons many people in the world today aren't enjoying the blessing and benefit of the sweet sleep that God has promised to His children. In fact, even many Christians struggle with falling asleep, getting enough sleep, and insomnia. That certainly is not God's will! God's will is for all of His children to enjoy a peaceful, restful night's sleep.

So if this is God's will, why do so many people, including Christians, struggle with insomnia and poor sleep? Millions of sleeping pills are consumed each day throughout the Western world, but often with little effect.

Of course, there are many different things that can affect our sleep. Some are natural things and changes that can affect us. There can also be medical problems or health issues that need to be checked and treated. But what I want you to see is that if God is the One who "*gives His beloved sleep*," then it's the devil who seeks to find ways to rob us of sleep and rest. The devil doesn't enjoy rest or sleep, and so He doesn't want anybody else to get any either. He knows that our effectiveness, our ability to yield to God and our will to resist sin are all influenced by the lack of sleep.

The Bible says that unclean spirits or demons go about searching for rest in dry places, but can't find any (**Matthew 12:43**). So a restless, sleepless devil, along with restless, sleepless demons, go around seeking people to harass, disturb and rob of sleep. They don't get any, and they don't want anybody else getting any either.

Now, I will admit, sometimes we may think it's the devil, but it is actually God who has waked us up. He wants to talk to us or get us to pray and intercede about something (**Esther 6:1**). Normally, the difference is that the devil uses fear and worry to rob us of sleep. But God wants to talk to us, and so we need to get up, read His Word and pray.

If it's the devil who is robbing us of sleep what do we do? First of all, we need to realize that the foundation for a good night's rest is knowing that God has promised us good sleep and rest. This is something that we should believe God for, and not just accept sleeplessness or insomnia as something over which we have no control.

Next, we need to remember that the Lord is with us. He will never leave or forsake us. Psalm twenty-three reminds us, "Even though I walk through the valley of the shadow of death, I fear no evil, for You are with me" (**v.4**). When we know and really believe this, it changes everything.

The apostle Peter knew what it was like to be in the valley of the shadow of death. Look at what happened to him and the other apostles in Acts chapter five.

> But the high priest rose up, along with all his
> associates (that is the sect of the Sadducees),
> and they were filled with jealousy.

> They laid hands on the apostles and put them in a public jail.
> But during the night an angel of the Lord opened the gates of the prison, and taking them out he said, "Go, stand and speak to the people in the temple the whole message of this Life." (**Acts 5:17-20**)

This is the first time Peter was arrested for his faith. He experienced God delivering him supernaturally from prison, and that was an awesome testimony indeed. And then later in **Acts 12**, we find Peter arrested again and put in prison for the second time. But this time the situation was different. It was much more serious. James, the brother of John, had also been arrested right before this happened to Peter. But an angel didn't come to rescue James. In fact, he was shockingly put to death by Herod (**12:2**). So although Peter was encouraged and had an awesome testimony of God using an angel to deliver him from prison (in **Acts chapter five**), what happened to James could have caused some confusion in his mind. "Why did the angel set us free the first time we were in prison and yet didn't rescue James?" Peter might have wondered. He spent several days in prison because Herod was waiting to bring him before the people after the Passover, the Bible says.

Knowing the devil like we do, he probably came and injected this thought into Peter's mind. "God delivered you the first time Pete, but it ain't gonna happen this time, buddy. I had James put to death, and so you better set your house in order 'cause this is your last night on earth."

The Bible says, "On the very night when Herod was about to bring him forward" for judgment and execution, Peter was sleeping. Isn't that amazing? "*On the very night*" before execution, he was sound asleep, the Bible confirms. Now you'd think that Peter would be sweating bullets with his eyes wide open, worried about what was going to happen to him the next day. But that wasn't the way it was at all. Even though he had soldiers chained to him, and others all around him guarding him, we find Peter amazingly sound asleep in the jail cell (**Acts 12:6**). The angel even had to hit Peter on the side to wake him up he was sleeping so soundly! How would you have been sleeping that night? How could Peter sleep like that, seemingly without a care in the world?

Well, first of all, in verse 5 it says that fervent prayer was being made for Peter by the Church. And although I'm sure some people were praying for James, it doesn't specifically mention it like it does here for Peter. The church was probably shocked by what had happened to James and, therefore, got serious about praying for Peter's life. One point that should encourage us is that their faith wasn't as rock solid as we assume it was. They had struggles in prayer just like we sometimes do. When the angel got Peter out, and he went to the house where they were praying, they didn't have enough faith to really believe that it was him, set free, at the door! But, thank God, the Lord accepted the mustard seed of faith in their prayers and obedience, and rescued Peter. The point I want you to see is that even if we feel that our prayers are weak, they can definitely have an effect on people and their circumstances as this story shows. So their prayers surely helped Peter.

But Peter also had to do something himself. I think Peter very likely had followed the Lord's example from **Matthew chapter 4**. He rebuked the devil and any temptation to give in to fear, and may have even reminded Satan, as well, of the prison that was awaiting him in hell in the future. Most likely he had also reminded himself of the promises of God as he and the soldiers laid down to sleep that night.

Peter was also now a man filled with the Holy Spirit. Before, he had denied Jesus, but now he wasn't running from danger. He stayed in Jerusalem and kept on standing for Jesus in spite of what had happened to James. So Peter knew how to walk in the Spirit and stay filled with the Holy Spirit. Oh, what a difference the power of the Holy Spirit makes. And, oh, how we need His power, boldness, and infilling today, as well! So whatever spiritual warfare went on in Peter's mind, the fact remains that God enabled him to sleep soundly in the face of almost certain death, and He can do the same for you and me.

Therefore, we have to get control of our mind and thoughts if we want to sleep peacefully every night. We cannot let our thoughts run wild. I'm sure Peter's carnal mind wanted to go crazy with fear about what was going to happen the next day. But Peter controlled his thoughts and trusted in God. Studies have shown that most people's unconscious thoughts are negative. In other words, their mind is saying negative things to them throughout the day. We have to recognize this, stop these negative, doubt-filled, anxiety-filled thoughts and then actively replace them with God's thoughts and words. The more we speak God's Word to ourselves, memorize God's Word, sing God's Word, believe His promises and what He says about us personally, the more we'll begin to enjoy His peace and experience sound mind.

So after we take control of our thoughts, the next thing we need to do is find Bible verses that deal with the issues that are causing us anxiety and fear. As I said, Peter was probably meditating on the Word of God before he fell asleep that night in prison. Meditate on the Scriptures throughout the day, every day. Fill your thoughts with God's thoughts, and God's Words. Listen to Christian praise and worship music, and other Christian music that brings peace to your mind and emotions. Give no place to the devil (**Ephesians 4:27**).

There is one last thing I want to mention that probably helped Peter to fall asleep that night. He had another profound experience in his life one night on the sea in **Matthew chapter 8**. He and the other disciples were crossing the Sea of Galilee one night and Jesus had fallen asleep below. A mighty storm came out of nowhere and was threatening to capsize the boat and drown them all. They were scared to death, but Jesus was asleep below deck. They were incredulous that Jesus would be sleeping right through such a life-threatening situation. They woke Him up and said, "Save us, Lord; we are perishing!" Jesus' words probably made them feel even more confused. "Why are you afraid, you men of little faith?" "'Why are you afraid?' Can't He see that we're almost dead here?" Peter was probably thinking. Then something amazing happened that they would never forget. Jesus got up and rebuked the wind and the waves, and everything became calm. There in the jail cell, he was probably thinking, "I'm not going to make the same mistake twice. I'm not going to lose another night's sleep on a stormy, fearful night. The Master, who slept through the storm, lives in me now and is with me. I have perfect peace." He may have been thinking, "The Lord died between two thieves so that I could sleep between two soldiers." And with these thoughts Peter drifted off into a sweet, deep sleep of peace. That is faith and trust. That comes from knowing the Lord intimately. So even though Peter was in prison and bound with two chains, he was free. And that's what the Lord wants to do for us.

It should seem obvious now that the area of sleep can become a spiritual battleground. War destroys and disturbs peace. The devil's spiritual warfare does the same thing. So you need to know how to guard against these attacks, and also root out and defeat the enemy who may have gained a stronghold in your sleep patterns.

I'm not going to delve much into practical things that can affect our sleep, but I do want to mention at least one. That is, not watching television thirty minutes to an hour before your regular bedtime. It's a fact that since the creation of television it has altered people's sleep patterns around the world. While we're on the subject of TV or any movies, we especially need to avoid any horror or scary movies. You'd think this would be obvious, but I don't take anything for granted anymore among Christians. Watching anything scary is just asking for trouble not only when you want to get to sleep, but in life in general, as well. When you watch scary shows or movies, you are giving the devil more and more of the ammunition he needs to plant seeds of fear and mental illness in your life. You'll be thinking about and looking for the boogeyman in your closet, under your bed, and doing things you never did before, just because of what you have watched.

The best thing to do is to have time meditating on God's Word before we go to bed. God promises to bless us if we meditate on His Word day and night. Try it and see if God won't bless you, and your mind and sleep won't be better as a result of meditating on His Word as you are going to sleep.

Here are some Scriptures that we could call "**God's sleeping pills**." If you take them, and meditate on them regularly, they will help form a foundation of faith for peaceful sleep in your life.

> **Psalm 3:4-5** - I cried to the Lord with my voice, And He heard me from His holy hill. I lay down and slept; I awoke, for the Lord sustained me.

> **Psalm 4:8** - In peace I will both lie down and sleep, For You alone, O LORD, make me to dwell in safety.

This was David's confession. He spoke it out often, maybe daily, in faith that he would have good sleep. Having a close relationship with the Lord, knowing our Heavenly Father, and that He is our protector, all give us a foundation for peace and rest. Notice how the New American Standard and King James versions translate the following verse a little differently.

> **Psalm 127:2** - It is vain for you to rise up early, To retire late, To eat the bread of painful labors; For He gives to His beloved *even in his* sleep. (NAS)

> **Psalm 127:2** - *It is* vain for you to rise up early, to sit up late, to eat the bread of sorrows: *for* so he giveth his beloved sleep. (KJV)

Looking at both these translations we see that God gives us both sleep and also works to bless us while we are sleeping. So it's not just good sleep but also the added blessing of God working things out for us *while* we sleep. If we stay up trying to worry and stress out over things, then we hinder God being able to work for us while we're supposed to be sleeping. It's ***while*** we are sleeping that He does these things for us, and not while we're stressed out and worrying.

Proverbs continues with God's promises and blessings for good sleep.

> **Proverbs 3:21-24** - My son, let them not vanish from your sight;
> Keep sound wisdom and discretion,
> So they will be life to your soul
> And adornment to your neck.
> Then you will walk in your way securely,
> And your foot will not stumble.
> When you lie down, you will not be afraid;
> When you lie down, your sleep will be sweet.

> **Proverbs 6:20-23** - My son, observe the commandment of your father And do not forsake the teaching of your mother;
> Bind them continually on your heart;
> Tie them around your neck.
> When you walk about, they will guide you;
> When you sleep, they will watch over you;
> And when you awake, they will talk to you.
> For the commandment is a lamp and the teaching is light; And reproofs for discipline are the way of life

When you spend time daily meditating on God's Word, then, at night when you are asleep, His Words will watch over you, and when you wake up, they will speak to you.

> **Proverbs 19:23** - The fear of the LORD *leads* to life, So that one may sleep satisfied, untouched by evil.

When you fear and respect the Lord as you should, it gives you a basis and foundation for satisfying sleep.

> **Job 4:13** - Amid disquieting thoughts from the visions of the night, When deep sleep falls on men…

We're supposed to be enjoying deep sleep. This is God's design and plan for man. In spite of "disquieting thoughts," we should still be able to get a good night's sleep.

> **Ecclesiastes 5:12** - The sleep of the working man is pleasant, whether he eats little or much; but the full stomach of the rich man does not allow him to sleep.

Having a job, and working on that job helps your sleep. Physical work and activity is good for us and helps us sleep better.

So don't let the devil rob you of another good night's sleep. Enjoy the added benefit of living right and walking with God. There is a peaceful sleep that God gives and secures for His people who seek and know Him.

4

HOLY GHOST DEMOLITIONS AND TAKING EVERY THOUGHT CAPTIVE

"We are **destroying** speculations
and every lofty thing…"- **2 Corinthians 10:3-5**
(Emphasis mine)

When a country is at war, they use all methods at their disposal to destroy enemy fortifications, communications and supply dumps. Their armies will seek to destroy the enemy's means of transportation, including blowing up train tracks and causing train wrecks. This use of explosives to destroy enemy structures is called demolitions. It is a big part of winning victory in any war. Peace only comes through winning decisive battles, destroying the enemy's weapons, soldiers, and also their means of propaganda. Jesus said in **1 John 3:8** that He came to destroy and demolish the works of the devil. For you to have peace in your mind and heart, you also must learn to destroy the works of the devil. He is our enemy. We are in a spiritual war against him and his forces.

One of the ways to destroy Satan's works is to learn what I call ***Holy Ghost Demolitions***. When we have been trained in using the explosive power of the Word of God, we'll not only be able to take captive every single thought but also destroy ungodly and unedifying trains of thought.

When I was in junior college (called community college today) I was part of a Christian singing group called New Jerusalem Railroad. We travelled as a gospel train to churches in our area, blessing and inspiring the people. But there are also demonic, evil trains in this world. One kind of evil train that Christians should learn to destroy is a demonic *train* of thought.

In the movie *Bridge Over the River Kwai*, the British wanted to not only destroy the train bridge that was built across the river, but also the train that was going to cross the bridge. We too must learn to destroy and wreck demonically inspired trains of thought that we may unknowingly have in our thinking. These trains of thought start with just one negative thought or little worry, and then end up becoming a full blown, twenty-car train of fears and anxieties running wild in our minds. We must learn to take it captive and destroy it. There are many such ungodly trains of thought, but in this book I am mainly dealing with worry and fear.

We are in spiritual warfare against the kingdom of darkness. We must be trained in Biblical demolitions. We have to learn how to use the Word of God as spiritual explosives to destroy the demonic fortresses the devil may have built in our thinking.

Second Corinthians 10:3-5 tells us:

> For though we walk in the flesh, we do not war according to the flesh, for the weapons of our warfare are not of the flesh, but divinely powerful for the destruction of fortresses.
> We are destroying speculations and every lofty thing raised up against the knowledge of God, and we are taking every thought captive to the obedience of Christ. (NASB)

The New Living Translation puts it this way:

> We are human, but we don't wage war as humans do.[4] We use God's mighty weapons, not worldly weapons, to knock down the strongholds of human reasoning and to destroy false arguments. [5] We destroy every proud obstacle that keeps people from knowing God. We capture their rebellious thoughts and teach them to obey Christ. (NLT)

The King James Version gives us another important word to consider in relation to the battle in our minds.

> For though we walk in the flesh, we do not war after the flesh:
> (For the weapons of our warfare are not carnal, but mighty through God to the pulling down of strong holds;)
> Casting down imaginations, and every high thing that exalteth itself against the knowl-

> edge of God, and bringing into captivity every thought to the obedience of Christ (**2 Cor.10:3-5**).

These three versions say we need to "destroy," "knock down," and "pull down" strongholds in our ways of thinking, and imagination. The Greek verb for these actions is *kathahresis.* It literally means *demolition, to demolish*!

With that in mind, my personal, free translation/paraphrase of verses four and five would be: *We have to destroy, demolish, blow up worldly, untrue, irrational, demonic ways of thinking, imaginations and thoughts. Also, in the midst of this spiritual war, we have to take these wrong thoughts, imaginations and lies into slavery, and force our mind to obey and meditate on Jesus Christ and His thoughts. We have to first do this in our own minds and then help others with their own thoughts.*

An imagination is something you think up. And in this case, something negative or in disagreement with God's thoughts about you or the kinds of things He wants us to dwell on in our thoughts. It could be something bad you might imagine could happen. When you dwell on fearful thoughts they often bring torment, and worry to your mind. We have to realize that this is of the devil and must be dealt with like a snake or a piece of dung on the floor of our house. We have to get rid of it! The negative thoughts may not be just related to ourselves, but also related to another person, church, family, etc... We have to realize that these thoughts and imaginations are of the devil and should be lethally destroyed with maximum spiritual firepower, zeal and weaponry. This is what spiritual demolitions is all about. After destroying these negative trains of thought, we also learn to make any wrong thoughts our slaves and put them in irons and prison. Don't ever let them out! Don't consider or meditate on them again. Make them captive to Jesus' thoughts of truth, peace and victory.

The Bible tells us in the book of Proverbs, "Watch over your heart with all diligence, for from it flow the springs of life." (**Pro 4:23**) Too many believers have spiritual logjams, so to speak, that need to be blown up in order to free up the river of the love, joy and peace of God in us to get it flowing again in their lives. Jesus said to not point out the speck in someone else's eye without first removing the log out of our own. (**Matthew 7:3**) If we don't deal with the logs, we'll soon have a logjam of bad thoughts about ourselves, others and life in general. We've got to bring in the powerful truth of God's Word to blow the lies, fears and negative thoughts out of the water.

Taking control of thoughts and worries can sometimes be one of the most difficult things in life to do, especially at first. But it must be done. It is something we have to do if we want to live in freedom and peace. The children of Israel had to fight in order to take the Promised Land that God had given them. God helped them, but they themselves had a part that God expected them to play. They had to swing their swords and shoot their arrows at their enemies. They had to shout even while the wall was still standing at Jericho. It's easy to shout when the wall has supernaturally fallen down. But it takes real faith to shout when the wall is still standing there staring you in the face. It won't come down until we take those negative thoughts captive, believe God's Word is true, and shout praise to God.

God told them to not talk at all while they walked around Jericho. This kept all the naysayers and doubters mouths shut. If they had been allowed to talk they might have said, "W*hat are we doing here. This is crazy. There's no way we can breach that wall* *and take that city.*" In fact, some have said that the greatest miracle of all was that they did keep their mouths shut during those times of marching!

A negative thought can come to any of our minds, but a negative thought left unspoken will die in the womb of our mind. Why did God tell them to keep quiet all that time? Well another possibility is that their mouths had gotten them into trouble the first time they tried to go into the Promised Land. They spoke unbelief. They told Moses they couldn't take it! So it could be God didn't want them to make the same mistake again, and therefore told them to just keep their mouths shut the whole time. Sometimes we just need to keep our mouths shut and then we'd stay out of a lot of trouble.

Learning to think the right thoughts and speak the right words, God's Words, is also one of the keys to victory in life. Your mind will tell you "*It's not working. This is foolish.*" And so the Bible tells us that *spiritual things are foolishness to the carnal, natural mind.* (**1 Cor.2:14**) Until we learn to fight in this way, there are important battles in life that we will keep losing over and over.

My wife and I were missionaries in Mexico for five years. After a break time of a month or so in the States, we were returning to Mexico and spent the night in San Antonio, Texas. We got up and left the next morning after breakfast. We put the kids in the car and we had gotten maybe three miles down the road when a thought flashed through my mind, "Where is the document pouch?" I looked down and it wasn't where I always put it. A sick feeling came over me. I immediately turned around and we headed back to look for the pouch along the road. I didn't see anything, so we went back to the hotel. We asked and looked at the restaurant where we had eaten breakfast. Nothing. We went back to the hotel and talked with the people at the front desk. They said, "You are still paid up till noon so you can go back into your room if you like." So we went back to the room. As I tried to recall what might have happened, I remembered putting the pouch on top of the car as I was putting one of our daughters in her car seat. In the distractions of getting kids and last minute things in the car, I forgot about it and left it on the roof! The bottom was, it was gone. So I had to do something. We began looking in trashcans in and around the hotel. "Maybe someone had seen it and thrown it away," I thought to myself. I went to the nearby gas station where I'd filled up and asked if they had seen it. "No", they said.

At this point I went back to the hotel and prayed. A couple days before, I had just been at a Missions Conference at Bethany World Prayer Center and heard R. W. Schambach give a faith-inspiring message about a blind woman getting healed in one of his services. And so, with my faith built up and encouraged, I knelt down with my wife to pray. I said, "Lord, you said that if we asked for anything in Your name, You would do it. I ask You to get our documents back for us. We can't get into Mexico without our passports and other necessary papers. Thank You for helping us. In Jesus' name, amen."

Then the battle in my mind began. Would I worry about it or stand my ground on the Word of God? Of course, the negative, worry-filled thoughts began to come. The devil would say, "You ain't never gonna see those documents again. You might as well give up now." "What are you gonna do if you don't get them back?" On and on the thoughts tried to come. But I stopped them, and said to myself, "No. Praise God. Lord, Your Word is true. The devil is a liar. Lord, You said You would answer my prayer if I prayed in Jesus' name." So I would thank and praise

God for the answer. The worries would try to keep coming back but I just kept praising and thanking God, and meditating on the promise. It was a very intense time of spiritual warfare.

We only had two hours left that we could stay at the hotel and that went by fast. Finally, I told my wife that I would go check one last time at the gas station. I asked the attendant at the counter one more time and this time he said, "Yes, someone did bring something in for you! After you came and left the first time, someone came and said they had seen you leave the gas station with a pouch on the top of your car. They followed you because they knew it would fall off. As they expected, they saw it fall off the car onto the side of the Interstate. They picked it up and brought it back here in case you returned looking for it." A wave of praise and excitement rolled over me! I thanked the man, and then excitedly went back to our car where we all rejoiced together at God's miracle answer to prayer.

Now, I'm sure that if I'd given in to worry and defeat, we never would have seen those documents again. But praise God, we learned that God's Word, even though tested by fire, is true! I share that story to illustrate that there is a battle we will encounter in order to stay in the kingdom of God, which is the kingdom of peace and the kingdom of faith in God's Word (**Romans 14:17**).

Many people are having panic attacks, and attacks of fear and worry. They are worried about the future and so many things. If we don't obey the words of Jesus, then we will become slaves to fearful thoughts, dreads and worries. Many of us believe **2 Corinthians 10:3-5**, but do we actually do what it says? Do we actually and literally control what kind of thoughts we meditate on or allow in our minds. Of course, thoughts will come and go. The devil does sometimes put thoughts in our minds. But we are the ones who determine what we meditate on or give time to in our thoughts.

Now before we take a thought captive, we must first recognize and discern the source of the thought, and then secondly, examine to see if it lines up with Scripture as something that I am allowed to dwell on in my thinking processes. We must ask ourselves, "Do the thoughts I am spending time on bring peace, joy and freedom? Or do they bring fear, worry and dread?"

Of course, there may be things that we have to deal with that may cause us to be tempted to worry. Paying bills you may have procrastinated about, getting life insurance, getting something settled that might be an unnecessary worry. We need to deal with these things as quickly as possible so that they are settled and resolved. However, there are many other fearful things and thoughts that *we think* we need to ponder and consider, but actually we really don't.

Likewise, we need to realize that the devil wants us to meditate on the worst-case scenario of what could happen. And the worst-case scenario almost never happens. Remember Mark Twain said, "I've seen a heap of trouble in my life, and most of it never came to pass." Most of the things we dwell on that bring fear, worry and dread, we should just cut out of our thoughts completely right now and not let our minds think on them for one second. If certain thoughts are terrorizing you, then simply refuse to think about them. Rebuke them if you have to, in Jesus' name, just like you should a demon that comes against you. Resist them just like you would the thought to go rob the corner store, or use the bathroom in your living room. Those are absurd thoughts and you wouldn't dwell on them for a second. We must train ourselves to do the same with fearful thoughts.

Once you have derailed the demonic trains of thought, you have to get on the right train, a truth and peace-filled train of thought. **Philippians 4:8** tells us the train to get on for meditation. It is a long train that will surely get us headed in the right direction to get control and victory in our thoughts.

> Finally, brethren, whatever is true, whatever is honorable, whatever is right, whatever is pure, whatever is lovely, whatever is of good repute, if there is any excellence and if anything worthy of praise, **dwell on these things** (**Philippians 4:8**). (My emphasis.)

The first word mentioned here in this verse, and the only one that I'll deal with for the purpose of our study, is the word *truth*. We are to meditate on truth. It's not accidental that truth is mentioned first. Truth is the only solid foundation upon which life can and should be built. Lies and deception are the devil's flimsy building materials. They lead to disappointment, disillusionment, fear, worry, and destruction. They also lead to slavery. Look at any communist, atheist, totalitarian government. They are all based on lies and believe there's no problem telling a lie in order to stay in power and keep control over the people. Of course, sadly, politicians in almost any country are this way now, but in America we didn't start out that way.

The devil is called a liar and the author of lies and confusion (**John 8:44; 1 Cor.14:33; James 3:16**). He doesn't want us to find out or know the power, authority, weapons and blessings that we've been given through our salvation and relationship with Jesus Christ. Normally when someone is illiterate and uneducated, they are much easier to control and deceive. But when someone can read and learn the truth, they are on the way to becoming a free individual. What we believe is based on what we think is true. Therefore, if we believe lies and deception, we can be manipulated and held in bondage much more easily.

So first of all, we must have a love for and commitment to the truth or we'll never really have complete victory over fear and worry. Why? Because lies and deceptions breed fear and worries. The fact is that most of the worry-filled, fearful thoughts that come to us never actually come to pass. That is a fact. That is what is really true. Remember, it is *the truth that will set you free*! Many times a little investigation will allay many worries and fears. That is not to say that preparation for certain contingencies isn't wise. I'm just saying that we need to have a perspective that is based on truth.

Pilate asked a question of Jesus as he sat in his judgment hall: "What is truth?" (**John 18:38**). The answer is found in the words of Christ to His Father: "Your Word is truth" (**John 17:17**). One interesting point to note here is that the Hebrew word for truth is '*amet*' (תֶמֶא). (Our word 'amen' is from the same root word.) In Hebrew there are only consonants, therefore there are only three letters in this word. The first letter is the first letter of the Hebrew alphabet. The second or middle letter is the middle letter of their alphabet and the last letter in the word is the last letter in the Hebrew alphabet, all signifying that God's Word is truth not only from beginning to end, but in the middle as well… "The sum of Your word is truth" (**Psalm 119:160**).

And beyond that, Jesus said in **John 14:6**, "I am the… truth…" The Holy Spirit is also called *the Spirit of truth* (**John 14:17**). So truth is not only the words of God found in the Bible, but truth is also a person, Jesus Christ Himself, as well as the guidance we receive by the Holy Spirit. The stronger our relationship with Jesus, and the better we know how to be led by the Holy Spirit, the more solid our foundation of truth will be. The Bible, our relationship with Jesus, and the guidance of the Holy Spirit are, for Christians, the foundation of truth and reality.

So dwelling and meditating on the Word of God is foundational for every Christian to have a successful, peace-filled Christian life. It is how we feed our faith. Starve out any thoughts of worry, fear or panic, and they will weaken and die. If you feed them by thinking about them, they will grow stronger and you'll end up getting obsessed with such thoughts. Don't give them even one nanosecond of time in your mind. Take captive those thoughts, and fill your mind with God's thoughts. The more you meditate and fill your mind with God's Word, the harder it will be for the devil to find a place to get a beach head and set up shop in your mind. Derail and demolish all demonic trains of thought! Amen!

5

THE SPIRIT OF FEAR

Understanding and dealing with the spirit of fear

"Please God. Get them off of me. Help me. It hurts." This was the moaning cry of the Mexican Bible student when I came walking up. All of the student body at Calvary Ministerial Institute in El Carmen, Nuevo Leon, Mexico, where we were working as missionaries, was having special meetings at the ranch La Biznaga for a few days. During one of the meetings this brother began having demonic manifestations. A few of the leaders were ministering to him and had called me over to help. He kept asking the Lord to remove the demon or demons that were attacking him and causing acute pains, off and on, all over his body. Different methods were being used to try to help him get set free. Finally, we commanded the demons to leave and he seemed to settle down. But I think we all knew that he wasn't completely free yet.

After another day or so we all returned back to the campus in El Carmen and resumed classes. The Spirit of God was moving in awesome ways during those days as we were experiencing many supernatural manifestations of the Holy Spirit among us. One day in one of my classes when we began to pray, gifts of the Holy Spirit began to manifest with prophecy, dreams and visions. The students were speaking out what the Lord was giving them and we were all in the Spirit. Then, the young man who had experienced the demonic attack during the encounter meetings began to moan. "Lord, please take them away. Remove these demons from me," he continued to groan. Suddenly I knew what he needed to do. I went over and told him, "Brother, the Lord has already done everything He is going to do in setting you free. Now *you* must cooperate with Him and do what He tells you to do. *You* must command those demons to flee. You have authority that God expects *you* to use." I told him what to say, and to command them to leave, with his own mouth, in Jesus' name! As I helped him, he began to speak and command the demons to flee. Soon he was totally free, no pain or desperation. Praise God, he learned a valuable lesson that day, a lesson that we also must learn if we are going to become the overcomers that Jesus expects us to be. That lesson is we have God-given, spiritual authority that we have to use ourselves. God will help us but He won't do it for us.

Paul said that he did not withhold anything from the Ephesian Christians. He stated that he had proclaimed to them "all the counsel of God" (**Acts 20:20, 27**). There is no way to completely and honestly help people get truly free from fear without dealing with the subject of demons. If you are a disciple of Jesus Christ, who wants to be pleasing to Him, and pattern your life and ministry after Him, then you must not only believe there is such a things as demons, but also be trained and learn to deal with them biblically. Jesus said that the first sign that would *accompany those who have believed* in Him would be, "in My name they will cast out demons" (**Mark 16:17**).

Now I'm going to assume that you believe in the existence of the devil and demons as revealed in the Bible through the ministry of Jesus Christ. When I was in college, some of my friends in a Bible class told me that their professor, who was a Christian minister and had a doctor's degree, told them that He didn't believe in demons. He had never seen one. One of my friends responded, "Well, I believe in Jesus, but I've never seen Him either." Needless to say the professor got upset. Ironically the professor had sadly been deceived by the very demons that he didn't believe in (**1 Timothy 4:1**).

Also we need to be reminded about who our main role model for ministry is. Jesus Christ is our role model for ministry. We are to pattern not only our lives but also our ministry to others after Him. That doesn't mean that we all will be in full-time ministry and live just exactly how He lived. But part of this does mean that the works that He did we can do also, at least in some measure. Jesus Himself said that we would do the works that He did (**John 14:12**). One of the works that Jesus was involved in was resisting, exercising authority over, and casting out demons. Actually, whether we want to or not, we will have to deal with demonic powers in our lives. As Christians we are in a spiritual war and therefore will be attacked or tempted by demons at times. So it is imperative that we learn to deal with demons the way that Jesus did.

Now, in dealing with our fears and worries we have to know our enemy. To win a battle or war you must first know who your enemy is. One of the enemies we have to deal with in life is a spirit of fear and worry. **Second Timothy 1:7** tells us, "For God hath not given us the spirit of fear; but of power, and of love, and of a sound mind." (KJV)

Before Adam and Eve sinned, there was no fear, worry or anxiety on earth. It did not exist here. But after they believed a lie and sinned, the seeds were planted, and the weeds of worry and fear began to take root. Then there was nothing left in their mouths except the bitter taste of the fruit of the Tree of the Knowledge of Good and Evil that they had eaten from. Therefore all fear and worry have their roots in believing wrong things just like Adam and Eve did.

And then also, we know that the roots of sin itself came from disobeying God. But even though all fear has its beginning in the work of the devil, there is a difference between a general feeling of fear and a spirit or demon of fear. Of course, not all fear is necessarily bad. There are healthy fears that help to protect us. Fear of fire, dangerous places and threatening situations are all what we consider healthy fears because these are situations that threaten our very lives. These healthy fears create physical reactions in us that help us to deal with dangers and emergency situations.

Another healthy fear is the fear associated with doing wrong, sinning. Granted, there is a measure of the fear of getting caught in this. Because when we get caught punishment usually follows. The Bible says that the fear of the Lord helps to keep us from doing evil (**Proverbs 16:6**). Normally, we should have a healthy fear of judges and police officers. Why? Because they have authority to punish those who break the law. God is the Supreme Judge. All true authority and responsibility to deal with sin and breaking God's law rests with Him. He is just and will deal with sin. Knowing this can help create in us what the Bible calls "the fear of the Lord." This is a holy and healthy fear that we all need, which will help us to live good and righteous lives. It helps us to avert our eyes and look away from a sexually immoral picture or scene. It helps us to not take things that don't belong to us. It helps us to tell the truth. This is a fear, the fear of the Lord, which we never want to lose. The fear of the Lord is actually part of our arsenal to help us overcome a spirit of fear. When we understand the fear of the Lord, and have a holy reverence, proper respect and fear of God, then we can rebuke and even laugh at a spirit of fear. Of course, the fear of the Lord is the "beginning of wisdom" (Proverbs 1). But the love of the Lord would be the perfection or completion of wisdom. When we have grown in the love of God, we avoid evil not so much because we fear the Lord, but because we love Him and want to please Him.

But sometimes these same healthy fears that protect us from harm can become unhealthy and irrational (not the fear of the Lord) when we begin to think and meditate on them the way the devil wants us to. You see the devil can bring to our minds thoughts, suggestions, and temptations. When the devil's thoughts come to our minds we have a choice. We can choose whether to think and meditate on those thoughts, or we can reject them and not allow ourselves to think on them. Instead, we are to think and meditate on God's thoughts, promises, and what He thinks about life and life's situations. Also we must realize that fear is often, if not always, rooted in what we are ignorant of, the unknown. If we don't know God's truth and Word, then we will much more easily think on and believe the devil's thoughts. If you continue to think on the devil's thoughts, fear and worry will begin to get their clutches on you, and it will open a door through which eventually a spirit of fear can build a stronghold in your mind and thinking.

Of course, if you don't believe there is such a thing as the devil in the first place, then you are already deceived, and he is the one who deceived you. Jesus Christ, while living and ministering on this earth, believed in and dealt with a creature called the devil. I hope you don't think you're more intelligent than Jesus. We are wise indeed if we believe in the things that Jesus believed in. Then we'll have a foundation of truth in our lives that will prepare us for victory.

Now a spirit of fear is a demonic spirit that specializes in or has a twisted, demonic gifting or anointing, if you will, in the area of fear or worry. You could think of this creature as someone who specializes in making spiritual horror movies in our imagination, or mental movies that invoke fear in people. They know how to instill fear and tempt to fear. And they know how to use traumatic events in order to find a way into someone's personality and thinking processes.

One story that illustrates how sometimes a spirit of fear can find a way into our lives is part of the testimony of a Chinese friend of mine named Su Ling. She was diagnosed as being schizophrenic. She tried to kill herself three times before she heard the good news of Jesus Christ, became a Christian and was totally healed. During one of her suicidal times she tried to drown herself by jumping into a big cistern connected to an underground well. After she jumped in, it was dark in the cistern but she could still see the form of a snake moving around near her! She began to scream in fear!

Now her story is a good example of how irrational fears can be. She wasn't afraid to try to kill herself by jumping into the well, but she was afraid of the snake! After she had screamed for a while and the snake had not bitten her, she finally realized that it was not really a snake after all. What she was screaming at was actually a cucumber floating in the water nearby!

By that time all her screaming had reached the ears of a passer by. He thought a demon was in the well and didn't want to look in. But finally he chanced a look, realized it was a person and not a demon, and then quickly called others to come and help him get her out. Finally she was rescued. But her story illustrates in a funny way what is often the case with our fears and worries. They are often misperceptions, or lack of knowledge and truth about the way things really are. How many times in our lives have we been afraid of situations and circumstances that in the end amounted to nothing more than a floating cucumber?

The acrostic of the word fear is a good illustration here. False Evidence Appearing Real (F.E.A.R). We are panicking and screaming until we finally realize that what we're afraid of is really just a floating cucumber after all. Also when we come to know who our Father God is, and that He is with us, loves us and is protecting us, fears and worries don't seem so formidable anymore. We also have a choice to use two other FEAR acrostics. We can "Face Everything and Rise" or "Forget Everything and Run." Be sure you don't forget everything and run. Face the fear and many times it will be de-masked as the imposter it really is.

Now we know from **2 Timothy 1:7** that God doesn't want us to have a spirit of fear, or any demonic spirit harassing us for that matter. God's will is for us to have and be filled with His Spirit of power, love and a "sound mind." A sound mind is one that is under control, and thinks God's thoughts. When your mind is filled with God's thoughts there will be no room for demonic thoughts. There will be no place in your mind for the devil (**Ephesians 4:27 KJV**).

My mother used to tell me that an idle mind was the devil's workshop. There is truth to that. Our mind should not be empty or idle. We should be proactively thinking God's thoughts, and meditating on God's thoughts. **Psalm 1** tells us that if we meditate on God's thoughts every day it will help us to be successful in all we do.

Second Timothy 1:7 also tells us that it if we are struggling with a spirit of fear, it is not God who gave it to us. In other words, it's not God's will for us to have it! We don't have to just settle for a life filled with fear and worry. We can be free. There is something we can do about it. The important point is knowing that it is not from God.

Next we need to realize that we can choose what we think about. Sometimes, without realizing it, we unconsciously resign ourselves that our thoughts just run through our minds every day and there is nothing we can do about it. Well, that is a lie of the devil. We can and must do something about our thoughts (thought life). Many people believe they have no choice and therefore have trouble and problems with their thinking, and their minds. On the contrary, there *is* something you can do about your thoughts. Actually God *expects* you to do something about it. He even commands you to think and meditate on His thoughts, and His Word. He will give you the grace to do it, of course. But He won't do it for us. We have to cooperate with Him in controlling our thoughts.

How do you know whether you are dealing with common thoughts of fear that come against us, or a spirit (demon) of fear? When you are dealing with thoughts of fear or worry that come to your mind, and you recognize them, are able to then cast them down, and refuse to think on them, that is simply a situation of dealing with thoughts of fear or anxiety.

But when the fearful thoughts have begun to control you, when they have developed into oppressive, obsessive thoughts, or panic attacks, then you are most likely dealing with a spirit of fear. When you have lost your peace and joy, and you are now afraid to go about your normal activities, then a spirit of fear has begun to build, or has already built a fortress of fear in your mind and thoughts.

Spirits of fear take advantage of ignorance. Fear usually grows or breeds where there is ignorance, and a lack of knowledge and truth about something. If your knowledge lacks a solid foundation, then it is subject to an assault of fear. It is still weak and vulnerable. So when we begin to learn and gain knowledge of the truth about fearful things or things that cause worry, then we can begin to resist them and overcome them.

So praise God we are not helpless in such situations! There is something we can do to get free! First we must know that we have authority to deal with such spirits, and then we must use that authority in Jesus' name to get rid of them. Then after we get rid of them, we need to begin filling our minds and thoughts with God's Word, and God's thoughts. His Word brings peace. His Word builds faith.

We know that Jesus' mind was filled with God's Word and thoughts. So when the devil came in Matthew chapter four with lies and temptations, Jesus was able to resist the devil and not be deceived like Eve was. In each temptation He encountered Jesus responded with, "It is written," and then he quoted and applied the Word of God to the situation. Finally, Jesus rebuked the devil and commanded him to leave. Now Satan himself is also a spirit of fear, as well as all other kinds of evil. And in the end of this spiritual warfare experience Jesus commanded him to leave.

There are times in our lives as well when we also must command fear to leave us. God won't do it for us. We ourselves have to use the authority returned to us by Jesus and command Satan to get out of our lives and thinking. Jesus used God's Word and commanding authority to deal with the different lies, deceptions and temptations He went through, and had to deal with. We must also learn to do the same thing. When we do, we'll begin to experience the life, peace and freedom that Jesus had, and that He purchased for us. We will know how to deal with the spirit of fear.

6

VICTORY THROUGH THE PROPHETIC WORD

"...He (the Lord) answered me, And delivered me from all my fears."—**Psalm 34:4**

It was 1992, and I was in Nizhny Novgorod, Russia. I was on a trip preparing the way for my family to move there with a team, have a Christian Music Festival and plant a new church. My team leader, Tony Foster and I were staying at the Oktyabarskaya Hotel on the banks of the Volga River. We had been visiting key managers and setting up plans and details for the Music Festival (Church plant) which was coming in a couple of months. We went to bed, fell asleep, but in the middle of the night I woke up and had a feeling of panic and raw fear come over me like I couldn't remember ever feeling before. I felt trapped and was breaking out in a cold sweat. I tried praying and also rebuking fear, but I didn't seem to be getting much better. I woke up Tony and asked him to pray for me. He did and then we went back to bed, but I still struggled with what was going on.

Then over the next few days I was confused by the feelings of fear about being in Russia, about living there with my family and about other similar irrational fears. It wasn't a fear or confusion about the will of God. I knew beyond any shadow of a doubt that I was in the will of God. God had made that so supernaturally clear in the previous months that I had no doubt of that. I believe that is part of the reason why God spoke so prophetically clear to me over and over before we went. He knew I would need the extra assurance to take me through some of the tests and trials that I would be experiencing in Russia, and this was one of them. This was a demonic attack that I had not experienced before.

Sure, you could call it culture shock or whatever you want. But actually it was much more than that. It was spiritual warfare! I had intruded upon a demonic troll's territory and he was trying to scare me away before we established a beachhead. I was on the devil's turf (He had controlled the Soviet Union for over 70 years.) and he wasn't going to let it go easily.

But another important point is this; the Lord knew there were weaknesses in my spiritual armor, and these experiences were exposing them. My armor and the fortress of truth around me needed to be strengthened. I lacked a stronger foundation, a spiritual wall, hedge or force field of truth, if you will, that the enemy could not assail. I needed a spiritual armor upgrade from what I had had up to that point. What I had was not bad, but it wasn't sufficient for the battles I was entering into at that time. My present armor and shield weren't getting the job done. Too many arrows of fear were getting in and striking vital points in my mind and emotions (**Ephesians 6:10-18**). I couldn't understand what was happening.

When I was a kid, my friends and I would often play football. When we tackled someone, we would sometimes do what we called 'piling on.' One kid would get tackled and fall down. Then all the other kids would pile up on top of him. Sometimes after the devil finds a way to tackle us and pull us down, he'll then bring other reinforcements and demons to pile up on top of us, and try to *keep* us down. He doesn't want us to have any room to breath. Likewise, during this first trip to Nizhny Novgorod, it seemed the devil and all his forces were piling on me, seeking to smother the flame of fire to reach Russia for Christ.

One day when we were at the Gardenia Restaurant, overlooking the Volga River, enjoying the view and some western food, I struck up a conversation with a foreign businessman. As we talked, the conversation shifted to the subject of living in Russia. He said, "Well, one thing I know, I would never bring my family and move to Russia at this time. It's too unstable, unhealthy and dangerous." Without knowing it, he, along with the devil, was *piling on*. Thankfully I knew how to recognize the devil's voice. There was no way it was just a coincidence for him to say what he said at that very moment. The devil can speak through others sometimes whether they realize it or not.

Amazingly, the same thing happened right before we moved to China a few years later. We were still in Russia at the time, packing up and preparing to leave for good in a few weeks. One elderly neighbor was sitting outside, soaking up the sun of the short Russian summer. I told him that we were going to be leaving to work in another country. He said, "Well, whatever you do, don't go to China. That is a terrible place. I was there during WWII. So whatever you do, don't go there." I just smiled and thought to myself how stupidly obvious the devil is sometimes.

But if God hadn't spoken to me earlier and made His will about going to China very clear to me, this man's words might have cast doubts into my mind. You see, we have to recognize the source of thoughts and words that come to us in life. Fearful, negative, doubt-filled words of unbelief are from the devil, not from God. So many times we just go through life and never stop to analyze where our thoughts are coming from. Researchers tell us that we have about 1300-1500 words a minute going on in our mind. We need to know, are they ours, from God, the devil, or the flesh? Once we recognize the negative thoughts, we need to reject them, '*take them captive*' (**2 Corinthians 10:5**), and then choose to meditate on God's truths and faith-filled promises.

Getting back now to my time in Russia. One of the fears that kept coming to me was the thought that after we moved to Russia, I might not get back home. I would have thoughts, inspired by the devil, of world travel changing and not being able to return to the States, and crazy things like that. The devil would say to me, "Everything that can be shaken will be shaken (**Hebrews 12:26-28**). World travel is going to be shaken, and you won't get back home." The devil knows just enough of the Word of God to try to confuse and deceive us. I knew this was in the Bible and that everything that can be shaken will be shaken. But I wasn't remembering that I was supposed to be building my thoughts and life on a kingdom, the kingdom of God. That kingdom can NOT be shaken. God wants my faith to rest solely on Jesus Christ and His Word (**Matthew 7:24-27; Hebrews 12:28**). When Jesus was tempted and attacked by the devil, He used the Word of God to counter-attack and destroy the devil's words that came against Him. He also used His authority and commanded the devil to be gone. At the time, I couldn't think of any verses that related to air travel. I was in the confusion and fog of spiritual warfare.

Of course, this was an irrational fear. The enemy always wants to bring to your mind the worst possible scenario that could happen and then convince you that that very thing, in fact, is what is going to happen. He will bring to your mind the worst-case scenario, and try to get you to feed and dwell on that very thought. Well, he is a liar, but sometimes, especially at the moment of an attack, we don't remember that. It seems and feels pretty real at the moment.

As I sought the Lord concerning these fears, I began to understand that my faith should not be primarily in modes of travel, the American economy, the American military, in anything, or any other person. I didn't realize that I was substituting these things in place of God as the primary foundation for security in life. In order to be unshakable, my faith and peace had to rest solely in Jesus Christ and Him alone.

You see, even though I love my country, America may not always be here. No country lasts forever. Just look at history. But even if it does last, it won't be the same. Plus, America and every country in the world are being shaken right now in many ways because they aren't fully built on the kingdom of God and His truth. So we have to know that God never changes. His kingdom is unshakable, and He will always be here.

Also, His Word never changes. Hallelujah! It is only that kind of security and stability that brings peace to a troubled soul. Any area of our lives that isn't built on doing God's Word (not just a hearer) will not only be shaky, but will itself be seriously shaken. If you feel unstable, worried, or fearful about a certain area or areas of your life, it's because that area isn't firmly built and established on the Word of God. It's just that simple. Face it, and make the needed changes in your life and thoughts. Get off the shaky sands of this world, and build all of your life on the Rock of Jesus, which means obeying His Word.

A few weeks after the hotel experience in Russia, I was back in the States, preparing my family to move to Russia, and we participated in what we call **Prophetic Presbytery** in our church. A group of prophets came and prophesied the word of the Lord over individuals, by the anointing and inspiration of the Holy Spirit. These supernatural, prophetic utterances would help to give guidance and confirmation in their lives (**1 Timothy 4:14; 1 Corinthians 14:3**). Prophecy is one of the gifts of the Holy Spirit that He manifests through His people in the church. These are *rhema* words from God, spoken through another believer to us "for edification and exhortation and consolation" (**1 Corinthians 14:3**). In **1 Thessalonians 5:19-21**, the Bible tells us, "Do not quench the Spirit; do not despise prophetic utterances. But examine everything carefully; hold fast to that which is good." These prophetic words don't carry the authority of canonical Scripture. But they are one of the supernatural ways that God still speaks to His people today just like He did in the Bible. As He says here, they need to be examined (judged). But we are to "hold fast to what is good," and not to despise prophetic utterances, i.e., God's supernatural, present-day communication.

One of the prophets in the group, Joe Roe, spoke that I would "go out and then come back and tell of what God had done." When He spoke those words, a dark heaviness was lifted off of me. That prophetic word broke the lie of the devil off of my life and set me free! It gave me the extra spiritual ammunition I needed against the lies of the devil that were tormenting me. After hearing that prophetic word, I knew in my spirit that I would not only go out, but I would also return and testify about what God had done. God had given me the additional, personal *rhema* word I needed to defeat the lies of the devil trying to torment me. I didn't have any more fears about not getting home after that. Thank God for the prophetic word.

Of course, some missionaries have gone out and didn't come back. I believe that God gives us grace and strength to face and do whatever He has called us to do, no matter what the future holds. Ultimately, we have to come to the place where we are willing to go and not come back. Brother Andrew has often said, "Jesus told us to go. He didn't say anything about coming back." We must come to grips with that statement and our will to follow Jesus no matter the cost. But the Lord knew where I was at that moment in my walk with Him, and so He gave me the comfort and encouraging word that I needed to face my future. He will do the same for you!

Now *rhema* is the Greek word meaning a 'spoken word.' There are two Greek words used to express the idea of a 'word.' One is *logos*, meaning the written word, and the other is *rhema*, the spoken or timely word. We need both of these in our Christian lives. Thank God that He still speaks to us in different ways today, just like He did in Bible times.

There is another point I want to add to this train of thought we are on. It is another key that also helped me begin to get the victory over these fears that had begun to plague me. This key is being humble and honest about struggles with fear, and then facing them. After we moved to Nizhny Novgorod and were in the midst of the crusade festival and church plant, many people were getting saved every day, and wonderful things were happening. One day, an American pastor on the short-term team asked me how I felt about staying. Did I have to deal with any fear about continuing on in Russia after the large short-term team left? I was tempted to say "No. I'm doing fine." But thankfully I was honest and told him that I did struggle with some fears. He said, "I can understand that." We need to be humble and honest with where we are spiritually, then face the problems we have and get the answer we need from the Lord for victory. God gives grace to the humble (**James 4:6; 1 Peter 5:5**). When we are transparent and honest with the Lord and others, it helps free us from pride. Remember, God gives grace to the humble. Others, who might have the answer that could help set us free from our struggles, might then be more likely to share it.

I remember a story one brother told. He was riding in a car to a meeting one day with Brother Kenneth Hagin Sr.. On the way, Brother Hagin suddenly shouted out loud "Wheeeww, hallelujah!" Then he looked over at the brother and asked, "Did you feel that?" The brother, not wanting to be perceived as unspiritual, was tempted to say, "Yeah, I did." But instead he responded honestly and said, "No. I didn't feel anything." Brother Hagin then responded with a sly grin saying, "I didn't either!"

Why did he do that? It was just a funny way to see how the brother would respond. It was a test for him! To get free from fear we need to be humble and honest with ourselves and others, and then get the help we need to be free. God gives grace to the humble but resists the proud. Remember, the truth will set you free! Pretending won't.

So humble yourself and be open to prophetic words and Holy Spirit guidance to help you. Of course, prophetic words must be judged, and we are mainly to be led by God's written Word and the Holy Spirit who lives within us (inner witness). They need to "bear witness" with out spirit. But did you realize that many Christians in the world don't even have a copy of the Bible to read? And even if they did, there are also many Christians who can't read in the first place! If you say that God only speaks through the written Bible, then you are saying that there is no way for God to speak to these people personally. In the early church most Christians didn't have any scrolls or copies of the Scriptures either. But the truth is that God has many supernatural ways that He still uses today to speak to people. If you don't believe in it, then you won't be looking for it. You'll probably miss it or reject it when He does choose to speak to you through these means. That is a dangerous place in which to be.

Prophetic words are powerful for breaking down strongholds and encouraging God's people, just as the prophetic word given to me set me free from tormenting, fearful thoughts. Just know that these are one of the powerful weapons and tools the Lord has given us to help edify, build up His body, and give us the victory. Paul said he wished that everybody prophesied so that God's people could be blessed (**1 Corinthians 14:5, 24-26**). May it be so, Lord Jesus!

7

PUT ON A GARMENT OF PRAISE INSTEAD OF A SPIRIT OF HEAVINESS AND DREAD

To appoint unto them that mourn in Zion,
to give unto them beauty for ashes, the oil of joy for
mourning, the garment of praise for the spirit of heaviness;
that they might be called trees of righteousness, the
planting of the LORD, that he might be glo-
rified. (**Isaiah 61:3** - KJV)

I was at the Sam Chatman Blues Festival in my hometown of Hollandale, MS one year. It was a time when I was hoping to see a few old friends I hadn't seen in a long time and also to make some new ones. One of the singers, John Horton, was singing the blues, talking about his problems or how some woman had done him wrong. When he finished the song, he said, "And it sho be's that way som'time." (Translation for those of you not from the Mississippi Delta – "And it sure is that way sometimes.") I was thinking about that later and thought to myself, "I'm sure glad that I don't have to sing the blues." Now, sometimes I sure feel like singing the blues, just like anybody else. But I don't *have* to sing them. I don't *have* to let my negative feelings or emotions rule over me. And then the Holy Spirit spoke to me. You get to sing the joys of knowing Jesus, and the peace and victory that is found in Him. Amen! That's right! I get to sing the joys. The Psalmist in **Psalm 42:5** put it this way, "Why am I discouraged? Why so sad? I will put my hope in God! I will praise him again…" You see, we all have a choice to make when the blues, dreadful feelings, and fearful woes come on us. We can choose to sing the blues, and sink further down into the mire, or we can make the choice to rejoice in the face of fear. Even when the situation seems impossible to solve, praise can help us to overcome. As we praise Him, watch fear flee and see our spirit begin to soar.

Worry can lead to a sense of hopelessness, which causes you just to give up. Sometimes when worries, gloom and a sense of dread settle over your life, you may think it's never going to change. It's been this way so long, and nothing is going to change. Worry and gloom work to steal our joy. Sometimes you just have to give a sacrifice of praise to break the power of doom, gloom, worry and fear over your life. You have to shout hallelujah even in the face of fear and the situation where there seems to be no way out. Sometimes you have to make yourself dance and make yourself laugh and praise God, even though that is the last thing that your flesh wants to do. And it is that very act of worship, in the midst of the trial of your faith that releases the power of God and breaks the yoke and bondage of the devil.

It was 1993, and I was in Izhevsk, Russia, where I found myself in a dire situation. We had just started a church in this post-communist, Russian city a few months prior, and now the city government wouldn't renew our permission to meet in the auditorium we were renting. The time for renewal passed and so we would have to wait for a few weeks before we'd know for sure whether or not we'd be able to resume Sunday services. I was really tempted to begin to worry and fret about the situation. But instead I decided to obey the Word of God. I got up and made myself begin to dance around my office. **Luke 6:23** tells us what to do when persecuted and mistreated. "Be glad at such a time, and dance for joy; for your reward is great in Heaven" (Weymouth's Translation). I made a choice to rejoice in the face of fear and worry. I sure didn't feel like dancing, but I made myself do it, and it was freeing to my soul. I even smiled and chuckled at how foolish I must look to be dancing a jig for joy in the midst of that trial. But worrying wouldn't have done me any good at all. In fact, I would have been sinning if I had given in to worry. You see, the dogs of doom are always waiting to pounce on you when things look bad or impossible. And sometimes we just have to make a sacrifice of praise (**Hebrews 13:15**) to the Lord in order to see God's fire fall (**2 Chronicles 7:1**), and victory won.

Praise God we were eventually able to get our permission to meet renewed. But for three or four weeks we were only able to have our cell group (small group) meetings, as we called them. When we finally were able to begin meeting as a congregation on Sunday again, I found we hadn't lost a single member. As a result, the people learned the valuable lesson I wanted them to learn...that our small groups were the most important meetings that we had. So I didn't worry about where we would meet, and what we would do. And because I danced and praised God in the middle of the situation, I was able to keep my peace, God kept the church, and our people learned a very important lesson.

Even if they shut our Sunday services down, they couldn't stop our church! Praise God.

Isaiah 61:3 says, "To appoint unto them that mourn in Zion, to give unto them beauty for ashes, the oil of joy for mourning, the **garment of praise** for **the spirit of heaviness**; that they might be called trees of righteousness, the planting of the LORD, that he might be glorified" (KJV). You see, if we aren't careful, if we don't learn to deal with worries and dreads the way God tells us to, we can end up with an alien "Klingon"(1) spirit, so to speak. We'll have a "spirit of heaviness" *clinging on* to us and weighing us down. We can end up going around with a nebulous cloud of gloom that hinders us from living in the joy that Jesus died to provide for us.

Now in order to overcome that and prevent it from finding a place in our lives, we have to make sure that we put on the garment of praise each day. We must not allow anything to cause or influence us to take off our garment of praise. We have to "keep our praise on" as people like to say today. Isaiah's prophecy is for you and me both. It is part of the heritage and inheritance that God has provided for all of His children. But just like all the blessings of God, we have our part to play in receiving them as well. We have to take these blessings by faith. So sometimes, and especially when we don't feel like it, we have to make a sacrifice of praise to God.

In Bible times a sacrifice, most of the time, would involve the killing of an animal and offering its flesh. Relating that to us today, we also have to put our fleshly, carnal nature to death and to make the choice to rejoice instead of to complain, worry, and fret. We have to make ourselves praise God and thank Him for another opportunity to prove that His Word is true, even in the midst of a difficult and trying situation. And when we do that,

God's fire will fall on our sacrifice. His supernatural power will be made available to us and help us to overcome no matter what we're going through.

David had his share of trials and tribulations. In fact, he was in the very real danger of losing his life many, many times. And then the worst thing that could happen happened to him. He and his men and their families were living in the town of Ziklag (**1 Samuel 30**). When he and his men were away, preparing to go to war, the city was raided by their enemies, the Amalekites. They burned the city, and took all their wives, sons, and daughters captive! The Bible says that David and his men wept until all their strength was gone from crying.

David could have easily gone into a confused tailspin at this point, thrown up his arms and said, "God, that's it. I've been serving You, trying to live a godly, righteous life before You all this time, and now You allow this to happen. On top of that, I've been running barely a step away from death for years, seeking to stay faithful to You, and now my wives and all our families have been kidnaped and our city burned. How could this happen? I'm done. I'm out 'a here. I'm not following You anymore." And what's worse, all of his other men were speaking of stoning him because of what had happened. So first Saul wants to kill him, and now his own men want to kill him. In their hearts, they knew it wasn't David's fault, but they were just so embittered by what had happened. Their flesh wanted to take out their anguish and frustration on someone, and he was their leader. The flesh always wants to put the blame on someone when things don't work out right. "How could he have let this happen to them and their families?" is probably what they were feeling.

But thank God David didn't quit. Thank God, He knew what to do in such situations. The Bible says that he *encouraged himself*; he strengthened himself in the Lord (**1 Sam.30:6**). I'm sure that he quoted the promises of God, but most likely he also sang a psalm of praise and worship to God. He reminded himself of the goodness and greatness of God, and that God specializes in turning what the devil meant for evil to good.

One important point to note here is that he had the idea to seek God about the situation while he was in the midst of encouraging himself in the Lord. If he had totally given up, and given in to worry and hopelessness; if he had said to himself, "They're gone. There's no way they are alive. They've probably all been killed or sold off into slavery," then he would not have seen the salvation of God. But instead, he encouraged himself in the Lord. He probably remembered that Abraham had rescued Lot and his family and got everything back from five kings. He may have remembered how God helped him to rescue lambs from the mouths of lions. Whatever it was, he sought the Lord and got the mind of God, and then was able to rescue everyone and get everything back.

Now the last thing David felt like doing was encouraging himself, and praising and worshiping God. But he made a choice to rejoice. He made a choice to praise God. And, as a result, he was able to hear the Word of the Lord and get all their loved ones and possessions back. It is extremely important to learn to encourage ourselves in God, and to give Him praise and worship even in the low times, the fearful times, as well as the tests and trials.

There was a time in **Judges 20:18** when Israel had to go out to war. In such serious times, they didn't just go out without preparing and seeking God first about how to do it. In response, God told them to send the tribe of Judah first. Why did God tell them to send Judah first? Judah, in Hebrew, means praise. When we are facing fears, or find ourselves in problems, dangers, tests, and trials, the first thing we need to do is to praise God. Yes, we need to pray. But we need to do more than just pray. We also need to *praise* God. When we offer to God the sacrifice of praise, His power is released, and He shows up in awesome and mighty ways to save, heal, and deliver.

In his book *The Cross and the Switchblade*, David Wilkerson, in his early ministry, was reaching out to violent youth gangs on the streets of New York City. One day he was surrounded by a group of youths intent on doing him harm. Did he scream out or beg for mercy? No. He shouted out 'Hallelujah' and praised God. When he did that, the pack of youths immediately took off and fled the scene. The Bible says that "God inhabits the praises of His people" (**Psalm 22:3** KJV). So when David praised the Lord, even in a fearful and dangerous situation, God showed up, and the devil fled in terror! The Bible says, "Resist the devil, and he will flee from you" (**James 4:7**). He resisted the devil with praise, and the demons influencing the youths fled in fear.

Israel was on the outskirts of Jericho (**Joshua 6**). It was the beginning of their campaign to take the Promised Land that God had given them. God's instructions were to walk around the city for seven days. They weren't allowed to talk at all as they went around over and over. They weren't allowed to gripe or complain about the strategy. Some of them might have thought, "I feel like a fool doing this." But they didn't say anything. They held their tongue. Most likely they still remembered how they had just walked across the River Jordan on dry land as God had dried it up for them. At any rate, they kept their mouths shut. But that wasn't the strangest part of God's strategy. God had told them that after they had completed the marching, a signal was to be given. Then when the signal was given, everyone was to SHOUT!

When you think about it, this seems like the most ridiculous battle plan you've ever heard. But God will test us to see if we'll obey. He especially wanted to test Israel because it was unbelief that had kept them out of the Promised Land the first time. Would they rebel in fear and unbelief this time? So God tested them to the max with such a strange, illogical strategy of attack. Shout at the city wall. Who had ever heard of such a thing? Nevertheless, when God finally said, "Shout," they all shouted, and amazingly the city wall fell down flat, and they went forward and took the city.

But I want you to notice. They had to shout a victory shout before the wall came down. It's the easiest thing in the world to shout when the wall has already come down. But it's another thing entirely to shout in victory when the massive wall is standing there mocking and taunting you. That is faith. Faith shouts before the wall comes down. Anybody can shout after the wall has come down. The test of faith is to shout when it's still standing there in defiance. But notice. It was when they shouted that the Lord gave them the victory. That is what I want you to see. They probably didn't feel like shouting a shout of victory. But they obeyed the Lord. They shouted a sacrifice of praise to the Lord. And when they did, that demonic stronghold was broken and came crashing down. Praise is a powerful weapon that we must add to our arsenal. To the flesh and carnal mind, it makes absolutely no sense at all. But to God, it is a mighty weapon of choice. It is the one that God tells us to use first.

In **Acts 16** we see the famous story, and one of my favorite and most preached passages in the Bible. Paul and Silas had been faithful to preach the gospel in Philippi. They had also cast a demon out of a poor slave girl. She was truly in a pitiful situation. She was a double slave. She was not only a physical slave to her masters, but she was also enslaved to the demon of divination that controlled her. It used her to give demonic, prophetic messages to people and make money for her masters. But look at the spiritual exchange that took place. She was set free, and yet, ironically, the people who set her free were later imprisoned! Isn't that another one of the amazing ironies of this world and the ministry in which we serve? Jesus died and went to the worst prison, hell, to set us free. He took our pain so we could be healed. There is often a price to see people set free. Sometimes you pay it before the fact, or sometimes after the fact. Usually we pay it before by seeking the Lord, then afterward with persecution.

Paul and Silas were not only willing to set the girl free, but also willing to suffer imprisonment and beatings to obey God. Not that they necessarily expected that to happen here, but Paul had seen it enough to know what could happen anywhere he went following Jesus. So they were beaten, thrown into the deepest, darkest, worst part of the prison. The jailers put stocks on their feet. You've got to realize that these guys were men just like us. Paul himself said that he had to "discipline his body and make it his slave."(**1 Corinthians 9:27**) He had to deal with the old fleshly nature. They were human just like us, so the last thing their flesh felt like doing was singing songs of praise to God. Their flesh and carnal mind probably wanted to scream out curses and complain to God about the mess they were in. Their flesh most likely wanted to sing a song like the song popularized on the old country TV show "Hee Haw."

> "*Gloom despair and agony on me.*
> *Deep, dark, depression, excessive misery.*
> *If it weren't for bad luck, I'd have no luck at all.*
> *Gloom, despair and agony on me.*"

Personally, I have often felt like singing this song. I have felt a gloomy cloud of heaviness following me around, trying to take away the sunshine of God from my life. That's why I love this story so much. It shows me the way to freedom and deliverance. But Paul and Silas, instead of singing gloom, despair, and agony, made the choice to rejoice, and that is what made all the difference in the world for them. They praised in their pain. They sang to God in spite of their situation and bad fortune. The other prisoners there had never heard someone ever praise God in prison, and in spite of their beating. All they had ever heard were screams and foul curses vomited out of beaten criminals. So hearing praise in the midst of pain got their attention!

But the most important thing is not that the prisoners heard them. The most important point is that God heard them. And when God hears praise in our pain and fear, or praise in spite of a spirit of heaviness, then He takes special notice and comes. His anointing comes. His power comes, and we are set free. By praising God in the extremely difficult and demoralizing situation, God's power was manifested in an earthquake that not only set them free, but also everyone in the whole prison! God will manifest His supernatural power in our praise, brothers and sisters, and especially when we offer a sacrifice of praise in the midst of problems and despair.

When they were literally at their lowest, they praised God. When we are at our lowest, that is when we can give to God the highest praise. Sometimes praying is not enough. Prayer is powerful, and God hears and answers prayer. But they did more. They added praise to their prayers, and that released a Holy Ghost earthquake in that prison. Begin to praise God in your prison. Praise God in spite of the situation in which you find yourself. The Bible says that God is looking for worshippers (**John 4**); those who will worship Him in spirit and in truth.

Another interesting point worth considering is that God miraculously opened all the prison doors, but He didn't immediately heal all their wounds. They had been beaten, and then, after the earthquake the jailer got saved and took them home and washed their wounds, the Bible says (**Acts 16:33**). God has told us that Jesus took our sicknesses and pains so that we don't have to bear them. We can be healed. But He also told us that we would suffer persecution. We would be mistreated. What is my point? They didn't complain that their wounds from the beating weren't healed. They thanked God for the earthquake, setting them free and saving the jailer. They knew their wounds would heal. They just didn't heal immediately. But they still praised God!

Often when I am feeling like complaining and getting down, I like to watch a music video by a young Japanese girl named Ami Sano. As far as I know, she isn't a Christian, and yet she sings her song with such joy and peace. And the amazing thing is that I don't understand a word she is saying. It's all in Japanese. Why would I listen? Because Ami has no arms or legs. That's right. She has no arms or legs, and yet she isn't complaining or giving up in life. She is smiling. She is encouraging others. In fact, she wrote a book called, "*Don't Give Up*!" When I see Ami, I quickly stop any complaining and begin to thank God for all that I have. I begin to praise God for all the blessings He has given me. I quickly shut down my pity party and praise God!

Now when we are experiencing difficult times, the devil tells God, "They won't worship You in that situation. They won't praise You in spite of their problems, that's for sure," just like he said about Job. Prove the devil the liar that he is. You see, sometimes the whole demonic world is crying out to see what it will take to make us quit, to make us give up, complain and give in to sin. God won't let anything happen beyond what we can take, the Bible says (**1 Corinthians 10:13**). The Navy SEALS go through a training called Hell Week to see if there is anything that will make them give up and quit. The devil wants to know what it will take to get us to quit and leave God, leave the church and His will.

What will it take to make us gripe, complain, run in fear and follow the path of the Israelites who died in the wilderness? They complained about the food, the water, and on and on. We have to make the quality decision that if they beat us and imprison us, we're still going to praise God. The problem is that we often gripe and complain when our spouse or someone offends us, hurts our feelings, or mistreats us. We get upset when our cookies are moved and we can't find them. We aren't passing the small tests, so how much less would we pass the major tests or severe persecution? We have to mature, grow up and become men and women of God. We have to learn to praise Him under pressure, praise Him in the low times.

The "*spirit of heaviness*" is like a dread, worry, or fear coming against us, as well as depression or a negative mood that tries to dominate and characterize our lives. Praise is one of the ways we defeat this "spirit". This heaviness, negative mood, even fear or worry in some cases, has a demon that in many cases takes advantage of and maintains the situation. When circumstances, self-pity, worry, or fear of the future get us down, a heaviness can settle over us and weigh us down. The power of praise can help us to shake off the chains and shackles of bondage, and set us free, just like it did for Paul and Silas.

We have to learn to dress properly. What does that have to do with it? We have to learn to put on the "garment of praise," the clothing of praise, instead of the "spirit of heaviness", gloom or doom we may be feeling. We're supposed to be the light, not the dark clouds or foggy gloom. God gives it to us but we have to put it on. We have to put our praise on. We have to make the choice to rejoice. We have to do it every day. Too many people are popping pills to try to help them feel better and be encouraged. I'm not criticizing those who truly need medicine for some health problem. I'm just saying that we should first pop or take some of God's praise pills! As I was writing this part, the Holy Spirit gave me the following prophetic poem:

> Shake off the chains of worry and gloom.
> Praise the Lord, and soon, yes very soon,
> You'll see the skies begin to part,
> and sun start shining in
> You'll hear the voice of the Lord Your
> God, and know He is your friend.
> For praise is your weapon
> to defeat the enemy
> Release praise from your lips,
> and the devil, he will flee.
> So shake off those chains
> of worry and gloom
> And the spirit of heaviness
> For when you are praising
> and worshipping God
> You are at your very best.

So start your day praising God. Set the tone each day before the devil has a chance to do something. We are called to be kings and priests to our God (**1 Peter 2:5,9; Hebrews 13:15; Rev.5:10**).

A priest offers sacrifices. Each day we are to offer sacrifices of praise to our God. He is worthy of praise no matter how we may feel. Begin to praise the Lord right now, and use your mouth for what it was created for, to praise the Lord. And then watch as the dark clouds of gloom begin to fade, and light of the Lord invades your day.

Footnotes:

1. Klingon – Name of a race of aliens in the Star Trek series.

8

SPIRITUAL PARASITES: WHAT'S EATING YOU?

WARNING ADVISORY:
Some of the material in this chapter will be considered very gross to some people.
You are forewarned!

Parasitos - (Greek) "*One who eats at the table of another.*"

I already know that many of you will want to just skip over this chapter, but I urge you to persevere through it in spite of the thought that you might get grossed out. Most people don't like to think about the subject of parasites because they get creeped or yucked out, but the ubiquitous creatures are actually much more a part of life than most of us realize. Parasites are everywhere and part of almost every living thing, including you and me. We all have to deal with them to one degree or another. What you may not realize though is that they are also just as real and prolific in the spirit and mental world.

In the natural world there are literally thousands of different kinds of parasites. At least 1.47 billion people are infected with helminthes, or intestinal parasites that reside in the human gastrointestinal tract. The U.S. National Parasite Collection is guardian of more than 100,000 types of parasites. Once I saw a picture of a parasitic fungi on the thorax of a housefly. The housefly had a parasite! Jonathan Swift said, "A flea hath smaller fleas that on him prey." So a lot of this parasitic activity goes on without our realizing it. The same is true in the spirit realm as well.

My in-laws were missionaries to Brazil for over 40 years and they would periodically give their children anti-parasite medicines or foods to help get rid of possible parasites they knew were prevalent where they lived. We need to do the same thing spiritually. There are many lessons in the physical world around us that have a parallel lesson for us to learn about the spirit world, where our spiritual warfare takes place. And so it is with parasitic creatures.

Spiritual parasites can be many things. But for this book, I've confined its scope to the fears, worries and dreads that often get into our thinking, our believing, and affect us adversely. They weaken us spiritually just like natural parasites weaken us physically. Spiritual parasites can also sometimes be evil spirits, or demons that oppress us in different ways as well. Just having these kinds of negative thoughts come to our minds from time to time does not necessarily indicate the presence of a demon. But if we become oppressed or even obsessed with negative thoughts of fear, worry and dread, then most likely that is an indication of demonic activity at work. Of course, demons are just like parasites in that they seek a host to afflict in some way, either from without or from within. They can harass someone if they are able to get into their thinking or possibly afflict their body.

My family and I were missionaries in Mexico for five years in the late '80s and early '90s. We would go out to the border every so often in order to renew our visas. On one stay at the border in Laredo, Texas, there was another family there with us. They had been on an outreach among the many different people groups of Mexico. It was very wet and muddy where they stayed and, as a result, their little daughter came down with a bad case of intestinal worms, parasites. She was very pale, anemic and had no energy. My wife, Anita, told them to give her a couple of spoons full of papaya seeds to eat. Our friend gave them to her daughter and the following morning all the worms came out when she went to the bathroom. She immediately began to improve and recover her energy.

Many Christians are in the same situation as our missionary friend's daughter. They have parasitic thoughts, fears, and worries that eat away at their spiritual vitality and energy. The Bible says that "the joy of the Lord is our strength" (**Nehemiah 8:10**). Parasites of fear and worry eat away at our joy, resulting in a pale and anemic faith without peace or victory. Only serious doses of biblical, spiritual papaya seeds of truth found in the Word of God can drive them out of our lives.

In the Greek language the word 'parasite' means "one who eats at the table of another." In **Psalm 23:5** the Lord tells us that He "prepares a table for us in the presence of our enemies." God has prepared a table for us in the presence of our enemies, which, among others, are spiritual parasites. Spiritual parasites include bad habits, negative thoughts, anger, lust, doubt, fear and worry. The problem with many Christians is that they aren't the ones eating at the Lord's table. The devil has been eating at their table, and they don't even realize it. And it's been going on for far too long. We're supposed to be dining off the spoils of our enemies who Jesus defeated. They include the world, the flesh, negative thoughts, the devil, demons, and all he uses to oppose us. We're supposed to be '*eating their lunch*' so to speak. But instead, too often it's the devil who is eating *our* lunch, bothering us, and feeding off of us. The problem is that parasitic thoughts and demons have no table manners. If you are a Christian, they want to come to the table of blessing and peace that the Lord God has provided for you, and then steal and devour it all away so there is none left for you.

This brings us to the story of Israel and their task of taking the Promised Land that God had given them. God had promised to give His people rest, peace, milk and honey in the Promised Land. But there was one catch or condition. They would have to fight and drive out all the opposition that was there to hinder and stop them from obtaining all that God had promised them. God had said that He would go before them and help give them the victory, but they also had a part to play. They would have to use their faith, go forth, drive out their enemies, and then actively take possession of what God had promised them. Israel's main opposition was found in a group of nations I jokingly call the "Parasites." Within this group were different types of "Parasite" people groups. These different people groups were called Hittites, Perizzites, Canaanites, Hivites, Girgashites, Amorites and Jebusites living in the land. Moreover, these "Ites" were much like parasites and would have to be forcefully removed.

Our destiny and inheritance also involves a Promised Land, but more accurately we should call it our *Promise* Land. Peter, as well as Paul, tell us that God has given us wonderful and awesome promises through which we can rule and reign as kings in this life (**2 Peter 1:4; Romans 5:17**). Our inheritance is to enjoy the benefits and blessings, the spoils if you will, of what Christ won for us on Calvary, and then also go forth and take our Promise Land in this life.

We also have "Ites" and parasites that are determined to keep us from fully enjoying all the milk and honey that God has planned for us as Christians. But too often, instead of persevering to root them out, some of us, like Israel, resign ourselves to having to live with certain dug-in "Ites" and parasites around us. But this is not God's will! God doesn't want us being hindered and bound by fears, worry, dreads and negative habits of any kind. These things that hinder, torment, and eat on us are those spiritual parasites that drain us of everyday life, energy, joy and power. They eat away at our peace. They eat away at our joy.

We have many different types of spiritual parasites to deal with in life. There were giants in the land that Israel had to deal with. But to many of you today, your parasites are giant problems that confront you as well. And if you keep feeding a parasite it will grow, and even give birth to even more parasites. So let's learn to ruthlessly deal with them while they are small, before they have a chance to grow. But even if they have grown, the Word of God and the power of the Holy Spirit are more than enough to help us drive them out of our lives, in Jesus' name! It just might take a little more time to completely root them out.

Bruce Olson is a pioneer missionary/apostle among the Motilone/Bari Indians of Columbia. He tells the story, in his book "Bruchko," of something that happened during his early years there. He was travelling one time out of the jungle, back to civilization for medicine, and had forgotten to hunt for food for the trip. After three days without food he was exhausted and fell into a fitful sleep.

He said that while he slept he had a dream. He dreamed about the jungle and it was full of butterflies. Then one of the butterflies flew into his mouth and got stuck, because its wings were wet. He could feel it beat its wings and struggle to get out. As he groggily, half woke up, he thought to himself, "There's a butterfly in my mouth. How strange. I'd better take it out." He put his hand in his mouth and did grab something. He started pulling it out. The more he pulled, the more came out. Then he really woke up! He could feel whatever it was struggling all the way out of his throat. When he got it out and looked at it, he felt sick to his stomach. It was an intestinal worm, about a foot and half long. It had gotten so hungry it had crawled up his throat looking for food! He said from that experience he learned to always eat something on the trail, if only to keep the parasites happy!

Now there's a spiritual principle we can learn from this story. The analogy is that the tapeworm inside of Bruce can represent unbiblical parasitic thoughts that often get into our thinking and eat away at us. Their presence hinders our spiritual growth. When we entertain our worries, dreads, and fears, we feed the spiritual tapeworms and they get bigger and stronger. They multiply inside us. If they are allowed to stay and grow, in some people they may eventually even cause mental illnesses. So we have to learn to not feed our parasitic fears, worries and doubts. Starve them out! Feed your faith instead. Feed on the truths of God's Word, then your faith will grow strong and the parasites will grow weak and die. In fact, meditating on God's Word is like eating the papaya seeds in the story a few paragraphs above. They will drive out the spiritual tapeworms and parasites. As you feed your spirit on the promises and faith-filled words of God, you will find that peace will begin to grow and settle in your spirit. But it may take time for the parasites to be starved out just like it took three days before the parasite came up Bruce's throat looking for food. Keep feeding on God's truths and your faith and peace muscles will begin to grow stronger, and fears and worries will begin to disappear, melt away, and even be driven out.

Of course, the analogy can be taken even a step further. The Bible says we can know the truth and the truth will set us free (**John 8:32**). Sometimes learning the truth, believing it, and applying it to our lives is enough to set us free from demonic harassment. But sometimes, just like Bruce had to pull the tapeworm out, evil demonic influences and spirits have to be cast out of people, as well as then applying the truth to our lives. Jesus had to cast out demons from people at times. Sometimes we have to do the same thing if we really want to help people get truly free. (**See Chapter 5: The Spirit of Fear**)

Parasites live either on or in the host. They feed, mate, and reproduce often either on or even inside their hosts. As I said, a demon also has the characteristics of a parasite. They seek to control, enslave and suck life from their "host" to varying degrees, and even use the host to attack others. Many Christians balk at the idea of the possibility of a Christian having a demon. Well, first of all, there's a difference between being possessed by a demon, and being harassed or hindered by one. You don't have to be possessed by a parasite to have one feeding off of you or afflicting you. The same is true with demons. Jesus came that we might be free, totally free. Not just partially free but totally free. Jesus said in **John 8:36** "So if the Son makes you free, you will be free indeed." Don't settle for anything less!

One feral fish parasite called cymothoa exigua is another example. It is an isopod. It swims through the gills into the mouth of a fish (Its worst victim is the rose snapper.) and destroys the tongue. It then anchors and settles itself in the tongue's former place in the fish's mouth. A demonic tongue transplant! This is such a hideous picture of what the devil tries to do in the life of a believer as well. It often doesn't happen overnight. It usually happens slowly over time. Sometimes it begins early in life, and is passed on to us through our families. Whatever the beginning, the devil eats away at our speech until fear, worry and negativity have filled our mouths, and we don't even realize it! Instead of speaking what God and His Word say about us, we say, "I'm afraid …" "I can't…" "I'm a failure…" "It's just too hard."

Our tongue was created to praise God, and proclaim the good news of the Gospel of Jesus Christ. Our tongue was made to agree with God's Word and affirm what it says about life and about us personally. Satan wants to destroy our Word-filled tongue, and faith-filled tongue. He wants to eat out our godly tongue, steal our confident confession of God's Word, and silence our witness to others. And then, he insidiously wants to replace it, like this fish parasite, with his negative tongue, his worry-filled words, so that we won't speak the Words of God, but instead speak words of doubt, fear, fault-finding, and failure. What is that wiggling around in your mouth? Is it a terrific tongue that brings pleasure to God and encourages others? Or is it a terrible tongue that poisons the environment around it with noxious fumes of fear, doubt, complaining, and unbelief?

In the book "Anointed for Burial" by Todd and DeAnn Burke, they tell the story of a man who came forward for prayer during one of their services in Cambodia. The man shockingly had sliced open the side of his tongue, placed inside the opening a tiny idol, and sewed it back together with the idol inside! "It controls everything I say," the man said, with a devilish grin. He later was cornered by three of their twelve-year old Christian students who were firing Scriptures at him. Fear spread over his face as he felt defenseless before them! Later that day, Todd and DeAnn found the man had given his life to Jesus, and he said that, after prayer, he couldn't even feel the idol in his tongue any more!

Maybe this is an extreme story, but too many western Christians also have their tongues controlled by forces other than the Word of God and the Holy Spirit. They have many times unknowingly yielded their tongue as a tool or sword of the devil that not only weakens and keeps them in bondage, but wounds and discourages other people around them, as well. We have to cut out and expel the spiritual parasites! Too many of us have allowed the devil to worm his way into our speech.

The Bible tells us our speech should be edifying, encouraging, and speaking life to ourselves, and those around us. But if we aren't careful, too often we begin to talk like the world. We begin to speak more about worries and fears, instead of faith in God and His promises. And so the fish parasite continues to live there contentedly hidden and anchored in the place where our tongue of faith should be. We need to wake up and realize we are not supposed to be complaining, whining, and worrying all the time. We need to cut it out, and transplant back in the "engrafted Word" of God into our speech. Our tongue was created to praise God, and speak the Word of God, not the doubts and fears of the world.

Just after we planted a church in Izhevsk, Russia, I was attacked with a strep throat infection. The inside of my throat became swollen, I found it hard to swallow, and finally my jaw was growing stiffer and stiffer until I could just barely open my mouth. I couldn't preach for the following Sunday service. Reluctantly I went to the doctor for an examination and help. She inserted a syringe into the back of my throat, pulled back the plunger to see what came out, and then showed me that it was full of pus. She said she would have to lance the glands to release the pus. I asked if she had any anesthesia and she said that all she had was a little antiseptic fluid to put on it. Then she confidently said, "It won't hurt." I was thinking, "Yeah right, it won't hurt you, that's for sure." Hesitantly I leaned back and she went to work. She took out a pointed scalpel and jabbed it into the back of my throat! As I was spitting out the pus and blood, I looked over at my Russian interpreter/secretary and she was as white as a sheet, leaning on the hospital gurney, about to pass out. Thankfully, I almost immediately began to feel better. The main source of the infection had been cut out and removed.

We need to allow the scalpel of the Word of God and repentance to cut out the sinful and infected areas of our speech. Then we need to train our tongue anew so that our words would become edifying, encouraging and faith-building (**Ephesians 4:29** - Don't skip over this verse! Look it up!). Some of us have been speaking negatively for so long we actually think it's humble and godly to talk that way. But we've been deceived by the lying tongue himself, the devil. Cut it out (the negative speech patterns), and begin to praise and give glory to God for His promises, truth and blessings He has given us.

"Pearl Fish" People and "Pearl Fish" Christians

We're supposed to be the head and not the tail. God doesn't want us running from fear.

One other type of parasitic creature that uses another animal in an unusual way is the pearl fish. You've heard of people who act like an ostrich that hides its head in the sand when its afraid, thinking that it is hidden, or that the problems will go away if he ignores them. Well some people take that a drastic step further and become like a pearl fish. The pearl fish and the sea slug have a unique relationship. When danger threatens, the pearl fish swims into the anus of the sea slug until the threat is gone! So he *ends* up, no pun intended, living a fair portion of his life in the anus of the sea slug. I actually saw this on a National Geographic show one time.

Now, I know some of you are saying, "You've gone too far now, talking about anuses and such." Remember, I warned you at the beginning of this chapter. And also, I didn't create these creatures. God did. There are important lessons to be learned in nature sometimes. And many Christians watch much worse things than pearl fish in movies and on TV. The point I'm trying to make is that many people, and even Christians sometimes, are like pearl fish. When danger comes, instead of swimming toward God and looking to Him, people often run to the sea slugs of life to find protection and security.

What are the sea slugs that people put their security and trust in? The most obvious analogies to this would be people who look to the Mafia or gangs for protection and security. Even worse, sometimes those trapped in human trafficking, because of trauma and abuse, begin to look to their captors (or pimps) as their protectors from danger and fear. These people, gangs and illegal organizations are the sea slug anuses of society. Communism and socialism are sea slug forms of government that seek to make their citizens into pearl fish slaves, trapped and dependent on them for the basic necessities of life. I've visited and even lived in Communist and post Communist countries. I've seen and experienced the consequences of such systems. It is literally like living in the anus of a sea slug. "Oh, but they provide this and they provide that for me. They protect me," some may say. Yeah, but you're living in the anus of the world. You have no freedom. And if you make the slightest public protest, before you can say "pearl fish," you're sitting in the deepest, darkest sea slug prison the world has ever seen!

Too many Christians are also cowering in the colon of cowardice, running from God's will and His commands for their lives. Jesus commanded us to go into all the world and preach the gospel to every creature. Much of the world still remains unreached and untold because we are unwilling to even peep outside our sea slug safe haven, and notice the needs of those without Jesus around us. Many Christians haven't even shared the good news with their neighbors across the street, much less gone to a slum area or unreached people group. We're pearl fish, colon Christians living way below the life of faith and victory that God intended for us. Now I know that sounds pretty graphic. But sometimes the only thing that can wake some people up is a shocking, offensive wake up call. You may not have considered this but a Christian living in fearful disobedience is just as gross and offensive to God as the pearl fish analogy is to you. But thank God, Jesus has made a way to set the captives free.

Deuteronomy says we're supposed to be the "head, not the tail" (**Deut. 28:13**), and especially not ***in*** the tail. You wonder why your life stinks. Wake up to where you're living, where you're hiding! Face your fears. Change your address and move out of the dark, confining pit that the devil and fear have driven you to. This is no way to live! That is not your destiny and it's definitely not God's will!

Jonah is one man who is the closest to literally understanding what we're talking about here. The big fish swallowed Jonah and as a result, Jonah lived in its intestinal tract for three days. If he had stayed there long enough he would have ended up in the rectum, about to become whale poo. And this is just where many pearl fish Christians are living today. What got Jonah out of his predicament? He repented and cried out to God. And that is exactly what we need to do also if we find ourselves on the stinky side street of Sea Slug Alley. Repentance means with God's help, to first of all, change your way of thinking, and then to change your way of talking and living. If nothing has changed, then true repentance hasn't taken place.

Jonah also called on the Lord to save him. This is another key because the Bible says, "whosoever calls on the name of the Lord will be delivered" (**Acts 2:21 KJV**)! Hear Jonah's cry from his dark den of despair.

> Then Jonah prayed to the LORD his God from the stomach of the fish, and he said, "I called out of my distress to the LORD, And He answered me.
> I cried for help from the depth of Sheol; You heard my voice. (**Jonah 2:1,2**)

Psalm 34:4 tells us "I sought the LORD, and He answered me, And delivered me from all my fears." You can be set free! There is hope and help with God. You can change your habits of talking and living.

Where do you run to when there's danger, fear or worry? Do you run to God? Is He your strong tower? God wants to get you out of that dark place, and into the light and freedom of His faith and truth. It's dark in there where you are. We're supposed to be kicking the devil's butt. Instead many are pearl fish Christians, living in it! Living in fear.

Pastor Mike Mille, of White Dove Fellowship, has said we "shouldn't be afraid of hemorrhoids or asteroids." We should be the ones giving the devil hemorrhoids. That happened one time in the Old Testament (**1Samuel 5:6-9, KJV**) to the enemies of God's people, the Philistines. We shouldn't be living in fear and worry. The devil will be the one who is worried when God's people find out how to live in freedom, and how to use the Word of God and the authority they have in the name of Jesus to resist him.

So don't run from fear. Begin to respond to it the way the Bible tells us to. Meditate on God's Word, resist and rebuke the devil, in Jesus' name (**James 4:7**). You might even have to speak specifically to fear if it persists. Why? Jesus himself spoke many times to evil spirits and even the devil at least one time (**Matthew 4:10**). If He had to, how much more will we need to, on occasion, command, in Jesus' name, evil spirits such as fear to "Be gone" (**Mt. 4:10** NAS77)! John Wimber used to say, "Treat them like a mangy, stray cat on your back porch, and tell them to 'Get out of here!" Begin to live in the light, glory, and renewed strength you'll have after you get rid of the parasites!

9

CONQUERING CLEAR AND PRESENT FEARS AND PHOBIAS

Fear never kept anyone from dying, but it has kept many people from living.

There are many kinds of fears that we have to deal with in life. Here in this chapter we will deal with a few common ones.

Fear of the Dark & Night

"All of them are wielders of the sword, Expert in war; Each man has his sword at his side, guarding against **the terrors of the night**." **Song of Solomon 3:8**

"When His lamp shone over my head, And **by His light I walked through darkness**;" **Job 29:3**

When one of our children was little (We don't remember which one.), during the night they felt afraid there in the dark, and in their bed alone. They called out, "Mama, come!" My wife Anita responded, "Jesus is with you." He or she pleadingly replied, "I know, but I need love with skin on it." We smile and may laugh at that statement but actually there was a lot of truth in it. We all need *love with skin on it*, especially when we are young. And thank God He sent Jesus to us, His "love with skin on it." Jesus, God's son, became a man (Love with skin on it.) to make a way for us to be rescued from the kingdom and fear of darkness, and be translated into God's kingdom of light (**Colossians1:13**). But most of the world still lies in darkness and fear of that darkness.

How about you? Are You Afraid of the Dark? Many people, especially children, have a fear of the dark. When I was a kid, I never really was afraid of the dark per se. There were times, however, at night when I was afraid because I thought someone, maybe the boogie man, was outside my room, and I could hear him coming to get me. Of course, it is the idea of darkness that works together with fearful thoughts that can cause us to become afraid at times.

But God didn't create darkness to be the haven of fear and danger that it has become. He created darkness and light to work together to give us the natural daily cycle of work, rest and sleep that we all need. So darkness doesn't have to be a fearful thing. It can and should be a blessed time of rest. And yes, sometimes the Lord will give us supernatural dreams. But since Adam and Eve's fall into sin, darkness developed into Satan's kingdom, which is called the "*domain of darkness*" (**Colossians 1:13**). It became a fearful place and a dangerous place that we need to learn to deal with scripturally. Then we won't be afraid of the dark or the things that sometimes happen in darkness.

Sometimes I have spent nights in villages in the Chinese countryside. There are no streetlights at all in these villages. So when the lights go out at night, it is extremely dark. Unless there is moonlight, you sometimes can't even see your hand in front of your face. So what do you do about it? Well, I always make sure I have a couple of flashlights. You have to have a source of light to be able to move around and make it out to the outhouse in the dark if you need to.

Job 29:3 says, "…by His light I walked through the darkness." If you are trying to go through life without God's light, the Word of God, you are going to stumble. You are going to bump into things, so to speak, get hurt, and also have trouble dealing with the fears and worries that attack all people.

Tibet Lonely Planet tells about a backpacker years ago in Tibet who went into a public restroom just after dusk. There was no light in the restroom area so when he saw the floor it looked normal enough. What he didn't know was that it was an open sewer pit, full to the top! He stepped out onto what he thought was the floor and fell in over his head! Thankfully, He was able to quickly climb out of the sewer, but not without having swallowed some sewage in the process! He also had to throw away his clothes and backpack. 1

In life also, many people have fallen into messes and filthy pits because they didn't know or refused to utilize the light of God to guide them. Similarly, if I had tried to walk to the outhouse during a stay in a village without a flashlight, it could have been disastrous. But thank God we have a supernatural light by which we can walk through the dark times of life safely, and come out victorious on the other side.

When we are born again we become "*children of light*" (**Ephesians 5:8**) and many fears are driven out of our lives, but not necessarily all of them. In the new birth, our spirit is reborn (**John 3:3-8**), but not our soul (mind, will, emotions) or body. We still have the same body, emotions, and mind. Of course, our mind has been renewed to a degree because we have repented. But our carnal mind still needs renewing (**Romans 12:1,2**). Sometimes we have fears that are deeply rooted in our minds and thinking, and we need help dispelling them.

Hopefully, most of us had parents who comforted us by their presence and with their words. Their words many times would dispel our fears. As we grew older and matured, we understood truth and reality more clearly, and that understanding naturally dispelled many childhood fears. So it is with the Word of God, and knowing the presence of God. His words of truth comfort us and dispel our fears. Of course, if there is a demonic spirit of fear troubling us, it will need to be run off.

One interesting Scripture related to fears in the night is **Song of Solomon 3:8** which says, "All of them are wielders of the sword, Expert in war; *Each man has his sword at his side, Guarding against the terrors of the night*" (*Emphasis mine*). This verse tells us that, in order to guard against the terrors of the night, we need a sword *at* our side. If the verse was written today, we might use the Word 'gun' instead of 'sword'. And, of course, some people today use a firearm as personal protection. But spiritual terrors and fears require spiritual weapons. We need a spiritual "sword at our side to guard against the terrors" that come against us, often at night. Thank God we have "the sword of the Spirit, which is the Word of God" (**Ephesians 6:17**).

Jesus used the "sword of the Spirit" when the devil came to tempt Him in **Matthew 4**. If that is the weapon that Jesus Himself used, then, obviously, we should use it too. We aren't stronger spiritually than Jesus. But thank God, even though we aren't stronger than Jesus, we have at our disposal the same weapons that He had.

The Bible also says, "greater is He who is in us than he who is in the world" (**1 John 4:4**). The Greater One is in us and wants us to be trained and equipped to use the same weapons that He did. Scriptures are like bullets we can quote and fire at the devil. The Bible is our spiritual sword that will help to guard against demonic forces of fear and worry.

One interesting fact from police studies shows that many times the threat of a crime is stopped immediately when the threatening person sees that their intended victim has a firearm. They don't even have to fire the weapon. When I was in junior college, a friend of mine told me that one time she was riding in her car down the highway. All of a sudden, a car with several young punks pulled up beside her vehicle and began harassing and threatening her. She said that all she did was reach into her purse, pull out the pistol her father had given her, show it to them, and they immediately backed off and left! Now whether you carry a firearm or not is between you and God, but we should all have spiritual firearms and our sword of the Spirit with us, and be trained in how to use it. Then when the devil comes around and sees that you have a sword and know how to use it, he will think twice before trying anything foolish. He'll usually just go somewhere else to try to find someone without a spiritual weapon.

One such sharp-sword passage is the twenty-third Psalm. How many of us have been comforted and helped by its verses? Verse four especially helps in dealing with fears, specifically, fear of the dark. "Even though I walk through the valley of **the shadow** of death, I fear no evil; for You are with me; Your rod and Your staff, they comfort me" (**Psalm 23:4** NAS). Actually, the literal translation for *shadow* is "*valley of deep darkness*." It can be referring to death, of course, but it also can be referring to going through a fearful experience in life or literal darkness. Why does it say we fear no evil? The Psalmist says because "*You (God) are with me*." Well, that doesn't seem to help all Christians very much. Why is that? Well, first of all, this Psalm assumes that the Lord is your Shepherd and that you are following Him. He may be your Shepherd, but you have to follow Him closely to enjoy His peace and rest. If you are going down your own path in life, and if you don't spend much time with God in His Word, and pray each day, then you can't expect to enjoy the peace and rest that only those disciplines can give. You aren't really following your Shepherd.

If He is your Shepherd, you also have to believe that He is with you. Do you really know and believe that He is with you? Is He more real to you than the people you see around you every day? It is this kind of relationship with your Shepherd-God that brings peace even when walking through the "valley of deep darkness." If you just go to church once a week and then read your Bible once a week you cannot expect to be strong when fears, worries, and anxieties begin to attack in the night. And isn't it strange how that is the very time when they choose to come? Often, right when you are lying down to sleep, any un-dealt-with worries or fears begin to surface and rob you of sleep. But if you have filled your heart and mind with God's promises and have come to know your Heavenly Father's protection and care, fearful thoughts and worries have no place to land on the runway of your mind. The more you get to know your Heavenly Father, His promises and His Word, the more you will grow as a child of God. You will eventually grow into a spiritually mature man or woman of God.

Generally speaking, adults aren't afraid of the dark. An adult will be aware of possible dangers in darkness, but won't have a fear of the dark itself. Why? Because he or she has grown out of those kinds of childhood fears. The same is true spiritually. When we feed on God's Word, exercise our faith and gather together with other believers, we grow into mature men and women of God who no longer struggle with spiritual childhood fears. The problem is that many Christians remain in the baby stage and don't grow as they should.

Psalm 119:130 tells us "The entrance of Thy Words give light." When we teach people the Word of God, and when we meditate on the Word of God, we are filling ourselves with light. Filling our minds and spirits with the Word of God makes it much harder to be attacked by fear of the dark. This goes for children as well as adults. When children are raised in an atmosphere of the Word of God, they will have a foundation of light in their lives. Then it's much more difficult for fear of the dark to attack them.

One apartment we lived in when my wife and I had only been married a few years had an infestation of roaches. The building was a quadruplex, and so if we used a spray bomb to drive them out, the roaches would flee to another apartment but eventually come back to ours. When we came home at night, I would turn on the lights, and we'd see roaches scattering everywhere. We'd run around stomping on roaches. One of the first words our oldest daughter learned was 'roach' because of this roach-killing rite we went through each time we arrived home at night. The point is that as soon as we turned on the lights, roaches would flee.

Most of us have turned over a big rock outside and watched as the bugs underneath scurry to get out of the light. Fear of the dark is like a big roach and will react in the same way if exposed to the light. If you turn on the light in a room, the darkness flees. And if you turn on God's light by meditating on His Word, spiritual and emotional fears will dissipate as well. Faith in spiritual truths is like a light that will also dispel the fear of the dark from our lives. In fact, spiritual darkness and lies fear the light of God's truth. Demons also fear the light of God's truth and Word. When you shine God's light in your mind and heart, the spiritual roaches of darkness will flee in terror.

My spiritual father, Rod Aguillard, says we need to learn to "trust God in the dark." God's promise from **Isaiah 45:3** is 'I will give you treasures of darkness, riches stored in secret places, so that you may know that I am the Lord…who calls you by name.'" We can grow to the place that we are not only no longer afraid of the dark, but also actually able to receive, from the Lord, treasures and riches out of darkness. The place that before brought fear now brings life and treasures of truth that set people free. Moreover, it brings riches in relationships, knowing that our Heavenly Father is Lord and that He is with us and will never leave us or forsake us.

Look at **Psalm 27:1**. "The LORD is my light and my salvation; Whom shall I fear?" God's light and salvation give courage and bravery. When the Lord is my light, I have truth. His light is truth. Truth gives courage and bravery. So light (truth) help us to not fear people. When His light and truth shine on my future, I'm not afraid. I know He has my future in His hands. His word also tells me certain facts and truths about my future. His Holy Spirit reveals others truths to my spirit about my future. So I'm not afraid. Light is shining on it. And so it is in every area of my life where I allow the truth and light of God to shine…where I believe and meditate on His Word.

Our salvation in God, also mentioned in verse one above, gives us courage and bravery as well. He Himself is my Savior and Lord. I don't have the same struggles with fear of death because I know that I'm saved, and I know I'm not going to hell. I'm going to heaven. This knowledge gives me courage. He is my Savior, the One who saves me, heals me, helps me, delivers me and so "whom shall I fear?"

Look at the rest of the verse. "The LORD is the defense of my life; Whom shall I dread?" God doesn't want us to have any dreads. He doesn't want us to dread anything or anybody. He wants us to boldly say, "I don't dread old age. I don't dread financial lack. I don't dread the college years of tuition and student expenses for my kids. I don't dread the future. God is my defense, my source and is bigger than any of these needs or potential dreads." Of course, this doesn't mean that we don't prepare for such future needs. My point is, we need to speak the Word of God, and not any words of dread.

Claustrophobia

Give me some space!

One time I was traveling alone in Moscow using the Moscow subway system. The doors opened, and the car that I was in began to fill up with people and pretty soon we were packed like Pringle's potato chips. When the doors closed, I immediately began to feel raw panic crawl up my back and my temperature rise. I couldn't leave because they had already closed the door, and we were beginning to move. The sides of the tunnel were only about two inches away from the glass doors. Panic was beginning to pulse through my veins. I immediately began to call on the name of Jesus. I also began to quote Scripture and try to take control of my thoughts! As I did this, I slowly began to calm down and was able to make it to my subway stop okay. Maybe you've struggled with such feelings or similar situations in the past. For me, I never knew that I would have a struggle in such situations until I was thrown into the midst of them. But that is the nature of fear and terror. They use the element of surprise, much like an ambush, in order to traumatize and bring about a permanent wound in the soul.

Claustrophobia is the fear of small, crowded or confined places. Many people struggle with and have trouble dealing with this type of fear. Now, this is normal to a degree because there can be danger in small, tight places. But when it becomes a binding, hindering force that keeps you from enjoying life, and fulfilling God's plan, it has crossed the line and become something evil.

Some examples of claustrophobia are being packed in the back of small vans, packed elevators, packed in subway cars under the ground, packed in small airplanes. When I became older, I discovered that I had trouble dealing with these kinds of situations. The places themselves didn't bother me. It was when they became jam packed with people so that hardly anyone could move that I would feel fear begin to crawl over me. I would have to start quoting Scripture like the 23rd Psalm, for instance, and slowly the panic feelings would begin to subside.

My earliest recollection of a hint of claustrophobia was when I was a child. I was part of a little league baseball team, and we were traveling in a car to a game in another town. I remember beginning to worry about how I could get out of the car if there were a wreck. I think when I was a kid I must have seen people on television trapped in a wrecked car or some similar situation.

One important point I want to mention here is that parents need to be very careful what they allow their children to watch on television or the Internet. Sometimes we don't realize the impact and effect that seeing certain scenes can have on small children. Television and the Internet are powerful mediums and can often make you feel that you are a part of the scene you are watching. Then add to that a small child who does not fully understand how to interpret or handle what he may be seeing, and you have a situation that could open the door to a spirit of fear. To an adult, a certain scene in a television program may not seem like anything to be concerned about, but to a child it could be a very traumatic experience. It could open a door to fear.

I mentioned before about a time when I was in elementary school and was hit by another claustrophobic feeling of panic. We were playing football on the playground. I had the ball, was tackled and landed on my back. Then everyone decided to do what we called 'pile on.' More and more piled on until I couldn't move and could hardly breathe. I started screaming, and nothing happened so I decided to do the only thing I could think of at the moment. Some guy's leg was over my face so I bit into it as hard as I could! Naturally he let out a primordial scream and tried to get away as fast as he could. Then a chain reaction of movement began until everyone got off, and I was set free. Now that worked as a kid, but it's not very rational or mature to start biting people on the subway or in an elevator when you feel claustrophobic. It's not going to help you get relief. There's no place for bitten people to go even if they could. Panicking doesn't help either. It just makes things worse.

Derek Prince tells the story about his first wife, Lydia. She was a remarkable woman, to say the least. She ran a home for orphaned girls in Palestine in the first half of the 20th century.

During that time, she faced riots, bandits, poverty, primitive living conditions as well as opposition from Jews and Muslims. But all during that time she seemed fearless.

Then one thing happened that surprised Derek. They had just finished a meeting where they ministered to hundreds of people needing deliverance and had seen many victories. They were returning to their apartment, but Lydia refused to take the elevator. Instead, she chose to walk up four flights of stairs. He asked her about it, and she said that she didn't feel comfortable using an elevator. She then related a story to him of how when she was a little girl playing in a cupboard under the stairs in her aunt's house. The aunt, seeing the door open, closed and latched it shut. Realizing she was trapped in the dark, Lydia became hysterical. She began to scream and pound on the door. Her aunt quickly came to her rescue, but in that short, traumatic moment, it opened the door for a claustrophobic parasite of fear to find a home in her mind. So after relating to Derek what had happened decades ago, they prayed together and commanded that spirit to leave her, and she was never again bothered with elevators.

Now I've already mentioned that biting doesn't help in such situations. That's pretty clear. Likewise panicking is no solution either. So what did I do in my situation to start overcoming claustrophobia? I knew that it wasn't God's will for me to be that way. I was in bondage to these claustrophobic attacks. It's not God's will for His children to be enslaved by anything, especially fear or panic. So, first of all, I began to meditate every day on Scriptures that would bring me peace, assurance and remind me that God was with me in any situation, especially claustrophobic ones. I meditated on those verses over and over again. I also commanded any spirit of fear to leave me alone and stay away, in Jesus' name.

When Jesus was attacked by the devil, He commanded him to leave. Likewise, I would follow His example and rebuke any spirit of fear that was attacking me and trying to keep me in bondage to claustrophobia. I thanked God that He was with me and that His angels were with me as well.

Next, before I got on an elevator or went into a confined place, I would claim God's peace and rebuke any spirit of fear. That way I made a preemptive strike, so to speak, against claustrophobia before it attacked me. I had realized that many times this fear would catch me off guard and unsuspecting. So I prepared by meditating on the Word of God, and would take Scripture cards with me as well as notes that encouraged me and gave me peace.

I also began to reflect on the fact that the possibility that I would get stuck in an elevator was actually extremely slim. Most people use elevators many times throughout their entire lives and never experience a problem. So I brought perspective to the situation. I saw it was irrational to think that anything would happen.

Another lesson was learned one time when I was on a small, confined commuter plane. I found that Christian music would calm my spirit and lift me above the fearful feelings that would try to overwhelm me. So I began to take an mp3 music player with me in those kinds of situations.

I would also prepare myself so that if there were a problem in a confined place, I would be at peace and able to comfort and help others. I changed my perspective about the situation. I began to look at confined places as opportunities to help others who might be struggling just as I had. I tried to get my mind off of myself and think of the needs of those around me. There could be others there who struggled with similar fears, and God had me there at that time to help and comfort them if necessary. So I would calm myself and tell myself that God was with me, and I was there to help someone else who might be fearful or uncomfortable. I didn't have as much of a struggle against fear when I was thinking about others, and not myself. This too is another key to overcoming this fear.

Once, while on a Missions trip with a team into North Korea, we arrived at our hotel and were told that our rooms were on the sixth floor. Our guide, also known as our "minder" (who minded and watched our every move), apologized that the elevator operator had already gone home for the day! So, without much excitement, we began preparing to lug our luggage up to the sixth floor! Just before we started up the stairs, the minder came back and told us that the elevator operator had returned. We could use the elevator after all. So four of us, along with the operator, got into the elevator. He pressed the button to go up, but the elevator when down instead! And it went down to the bottom, the very bottom. For the four of us, this was the lowest point of the trip (Sorry, I couldn't resist the joke.). The doors opened, and we were staring at a concrete wall in front of us! "Oh great," I thought. "Stuck in a North Korean elevator." Well, at least everybody knew where we were, and the operator was with us. More importantly God was with us. As the operator worked with the elevator buttons, I began to direct my thoughts to God's Word. Just then the elevator began to rise. Thank God! As we went up however, we realized the floor indicator light was not working. We couldn't tell which floor we were on. That's when we noticed that the operator was looking through the cracks between the doors and counting until we made it to the sixth floor.

Praise God I made it as well as I did through that situation, although I was startled when the elevator opened to the concrete wall! Here are some of the Scriptures I regularly meditate on that helped me to overcome claustrophobia, and maintain my deliverance from it.

> **2 Timothy 1:7** - "For God has not given us a spirit of timidity [fear], but of power and love and discipline."

I would speak this verse over myself. I would rebuke any spirit of fear or panic. I would say, "I have a spirit of power, love, , and a sound, peaceful mind. I reject and refuse any fearful thoughts." I would refuse to consider or ponder a fearful thought for even a nano-second. I would only consider and think about God's verses and words. Using the Word of God in this manner is what is meant by "taking every thought captive" (**2 Corinthians 10:4,5**).

> **James 4:7** – "Submit therefore to God. Resist the devil and he will flee from you."

I would say to myself, "**James 4:7** says that when I resist the devil and any spirit of fear, it must flee." I would use the phrase 'it is written' like Jesus did when He was tempted. I would say, "It is written, 'In Jesus' name that I would make demons go away'" (**Mark 16:17**).

> **Genesis 8:1** – "But God remembered Noah."

I'm sure that Noah got tired of all those many days in the ark. He and his family probably felt a little cabin fever. They were cramped, and possibly even struggled with fears and claustrophobia at times all closed up in the crowded ark. But God didn't forget Noah, and he doesn't forget us either. He is with us. When I'd be on a small commuter type airplane, I'd not think about the cramped quarters. I'd thank God that He remembered me, that I had a seat on the ark and could enjoy what comforts there were on the plane.

Paul & Silas praised Him in prison (**Acts 16**). You may literally be in prison, or feel imprisoned by different worries and fears of life. Praise God in the situation. The Bible says that God *inhabits the praises of His people* (**Psalm 22:3** KJV). When we praise God He will fill the situation with His presence and peace. As I mentioned before, listening to praise and worship music will help us to do this as well.

I still meditate on these verses and strengthen my faith in these areas as much and as often as I need to. I may have eaten a steak before, but I don't turn it down if I get another chance. It is good food. I also need to feed regularly on verses like these that keep my faith strong where I need it. If we don't use a muscle, it grows weak. The same is true with our faith.

Jude 20 also reveals a vital secret to overcoming fears. It is a very important truth that many Christians are lacking. "Building yourselves up on your most holy faith, praying in the Holy Spirit." I have found that praying in the Holy Spirit calms and short circuits the fears that try to attack me.

What is "praying in the Holy Spirit?" Well, first of all, praying in the Holy Spirit is Spirit-led prayer, praying the things the Holy Spirit leads us to pray. But also, more specifically, praying in the Holy Spirit is what the Bible calls, praying supernaturally in other tongues, languages, like the believers did in the New Testament. In **First Corinthians 14:14, 15** Paul states "For if I pray in a tongue, my spirit prays, but my mind is unfruitful. What is the outcome then? I will pray with the spirit and I will pray with the mind also; I will sing with the spirit and I will sing with the mind also." When we pray in tongues our spirit, by the Holy Spirit in us, prays. The Bible states that this kind of prayer *builds us up on our faith*. It builds faith and courage in us.

We receive this kind of prayer and the ability to pray this way when we are fully baptized in the Holy Spirit, just as the apostles and Christians were throughout the book of Acts. Now, I know that some of you may feel afraid at the thought of speaking in tongues. You have heard pastors speak against it, make fun of it and reject it as something done away with. But even the apostle Paul, the Christian we all look up to, said, "I speak in tongues more than you all" (**1 Cor. 14:18**). He said, "Forbid not to speak in tongues" (**1 Corinthians 14:39**). He sought for young believers to be filled with the Holy Spirit and speak with other tongues (**Acts 19**). He wanted them to be "built up" as much as possible.

And by the way, if you are afraid of speaking in tongues (prayer language), where did that fear come from? Have you thought about that? This book is about getting free from fear. Many Christians are afraid of the Holy Spirit. How sad and tragic. What deception! Where do think that fear came from? Did it come from God or the devil? Did it come from someone telling you truth or error? I have had to help many Christians get free from a demonic fear of the Holy Spirit because their church leaders had a fear about the ministry of the third person of the Trinity, and passed that fear along to their congregation! The ministry of the Holy Spirit is ignored and attacked so much because the devil is afraid of the Holy Spirit, His power, and the thought of Him filling all believers of Jesus Christ. And so Satan does everything he can to hinder the church from fully embracing the Holy Spirit's ministry. Luke wrote to help those attacked by demonic fear over receiving the Holy Spirit.

> "Now suppose one of you fathers is asked by his son for a fish; he will not give him a snake instead of a fish, will he?
> "Or if he is asked for an egg, he will not give him a scorpion, will he?
> "If you then, being evil, know how to give good gifts to your children, how much more will your heavenly Father give the Holy Spirit to those who ask Him?" (**Luke 11:11-13**)

Your Heavenly Father is not going to allow or give you a snake or a scorpion when you ask for and seek the filling of the Holy Spirit. He knows how to give good gifts, and especially the Holy Spirit, better than all the best earthly fathers put together. God the Father doesn't fear the Holy Spirit or this supernatural prayer language. God the Father created this prayer language and the Bible says that Jesus is the One who baptizes in the Holy Spirit. Peter, Paul, John and Mary, the mother of Jesus, would all be so shocked at how the devil has deceived and robbed so much of the church, for so many years, from the complete filling of the Holy Spirit.

Today, the largest and fastest growing segment of Christianity in the world is Charismatic, Pentecostal. The church by in large is finally rejecting that old, thoroughly debunked carnard of the devil that says that the gifts of the Spirit and miracles were done away with. Don't let the Devil rob you of all that's available in Christ.

But the Lord won't force this on anyone. It is only for those who are hungry to be worshippers of God in spirit and truth (**John 4**). I'm just sharing with you the things that have truly helped me overcome fears. It certainly made a big difference in Peter, Paul and the New Testament church.

Before I get on an elevator, and while I'm on it (if I need to), I pray in tongues. I have found a supernatural peace come over me as I do this. I fully believe that as I do this, my spirit is communicating with God in a powerful way and building me up. And thank God, it works. God's Word is true.

Now I declare that I am "claustro-courageous." I have claustro-courage. Greater is He who lives in me than he who is in the world! And He's greater than any fear that is in the world!

Fear of Man

> *The fear of man brings a snare, But he who trusts in the LORD will be exalted.* **Proverbs 29:25**

We know how Peter had shamefully denied Jesus. We also know how Jesus restored him. And then, shortly thereafter, Peter was filled with the Holy Spirit. He then preached fearlessly on the day of Pentecost and testified boldly before the Jewish leaders after his arrest. He was truly a new man filled with the power and boldness of the Holy Spirit. But just because you've had some victories over fear of man doesn't mean that there won't be any more battles. In the book of Galatians we are told that false Jewish brethren, who held the legalistic teaching that you have to become Jewish and be circumcised in order to be saved, came to Antioch to check out the Gentile believers. Before they came, Peter ate freely with the Gentile Christians. But after the legalistic, false brethren came, Peter fearfully and timidly stopped eating with the Gentile believers. He was intimidated and afraid of the criticism and rebuke of the Jews from Jerusalem. Jews weren't supposed to eat with Gentiles according to Jewish teaching. The Bible says that Paul had to correct Peter in front of everyone in order to make clear the truth of the gospel (**Galatians 2:3-14**). And Peter had to repent of not being honest, and also for being a coward. How could a man, who before was so mightily used of God, fall into such a weak state? Such is the power of the fear of man, if we are not careful.

The fear of man kept the children of Israel out of the Promised Land for forty years. Think about that. And it will keep us out of God's Promised Land that He has planned for us as well. Remember the story? God told Moses to choose twelve spies, one from each tribe of Israel to go in and check out the land and the cities that they were going to conquer. We find it in Numbers chapter thirteen. Now this was not only a reconnaissance mission, but also a test. It was a test for the spies who were representatives of each tribe. It was a test for the tribes as well. We don't often realize it, but the tasks which God gives to us to accomplish are not only work that He has for us, but also a test of our faith and character. And we'll be rewarded or disciplined accordingly.

So the twelve spies went out and checked the land, and its people. After forty days (the Bible number for testing), they returned to report back to Moses. The Bible says that ten of the spies gave a bad report (**Numbers 13:32**). What did they say that was bad? They said that they could not defeat the inhabitants of the land and take it from them, even though God had said that He had given it to them. It was a report of doubt and unbelief.

Now to fully appreciate what happened here and avoid the same mistake, let's look a little deeper.

First of all, they said that the descendants of Anak, the Nephilim, were there, as well as many other different people groups. The descendants of Anak were giants. They were extremely large men, similar to the giant Goliath, whom David later killed. When ten of the spies saw these huge men and their fortified cities, their hearts melted. Why? They were ruled by the fear of man, albeit giant men. Some people are intimidated by the giant intellects, bank accounts, or giant anger of others. In this case it was the size of the men that intimidated and struck fear into the hearts of the ten spies. It says in verse thirty-three that "we became like grasshoppers in our own sight, and so we were in their sight." Now this is an inferiority complex gone wild. But before we condemn them from our easy chairs, we need to remember what they were about to have to do. These ten men knew that this land was not going to just fall into their laps like a ripe apple. They were going to have to fight the men of Canaan in hand-to-hand combat with swords, knives, bows, and arrows. When they looked at themselves and compared themselves with their enemies, they were totally demoralized. And if we only look at the natural circumstances around us, the exact, same thing will happen to us.

But there were two other spies who had a different spirit in them, Joshua and Caleb. They strongly disagreed with the ten. They boldly spoke out that everyone "should by all means go up and take possession of" the land, and said that they would "surely overcome it" (**Numbers 13:30**). So that's about 80% opposed and 20% agreed. It might be that in such situations today, involving believing God's Word, the percentages would be the same. The question is of which group are you going to be a part?

Joshua and Caleb saw the very same giants, along with their intimidating fortifications. What made the difference in their lives? Well, the first thing was their concept and vision of God. How is it that they didn't fear these giant men? To Joshua and Caleb, God was infinitely bigger and stronger than the sons of Anak. They still remembered how God had used the mighty judgment miracles against Egypt. They remembered how God had held back the waters of the Red Sea for them. Those were the same waters that later destroyed the entire Egyptian army.

When I was in college, some of our textbooks and Bible professors taught us that the Red Sea was actually the Reed Sea and that it was only a foot deep! They were somehow trying to cast doubt on the veracity of God's Word. And yet, even if it was the Reed Sea, they somehow didn't realize that it was an even greater miracle that the entire Egyptian army drowned in a foot of water!

But Joshua and Caleb remembered this great miracle and also how God used a pillar of fire at night and a pillar of cloud by day to guide them. Through all they had seen and experienced, they feared God, and not man or his mighty armies. They had seen and remembered what God had done to such a big, powerful, fearful and intimidating army. They also remembered the promises of God that He had given them the land!

Joshua and Caleb also didn't look at themselves, and then measure their chances in battle. They measured the giants against their great God, Yahweh, and so there was absolutely no comparison. They also knew that God was with them and would not forsake them.

What the other ten spies didn't realize was what their descendants would find out forty years later. One generation later, their descendants would find out that those same giants had heard of the mighty miracles that God had done for Israel and were shaking in their boots (**Joshua 2:9-11**)! So although the giants were bigger and stronger physically, they were the ones who were in fear, and afraid of the twelve spies and all their people! That means the ten fearful, unbelieving spies actually believed a lie. They allowed their enemies to be taken out of the jaws of defeat because they believed a lie. Can you see how tragic it can be to be ruled by the fear of man?

We must remember that the Lord Jesus also promised to be with us forever and never forsake us. We need to meditate on the truths of God's Word and who He is so that our concept of God can grow strong. We need to know and believe that He is just the same Deliverer today as He was in Joshua and Caleb's day. In fact, if He has changed in any way, we would have to say that He is greater and stronger toward us in our time than He was for them in their time. How could that be? It could be, can be and is because we have a better covenant, based on better promises than what Joshua and Caleb had (**Hebrews 8:6**).

We also need to understand and believe **1 John 4:4**. "You are from God, little children, and have overcome them; because greater is He who is in you than he who is in the world." God is not only greater than your problem or any demonic force that may come against you. He is also in you to help you overcome the fear of man. We don't have to go through life with feelings of intimidation when we are around certain people or about to face certain situations. Feeling intimidated by certain people shows that we fear them to some degree. Intimidation and fear are related. **Revelation 12:11** explains to us some truths that can help us to overcome the fear of man and intimidation. It says, "And they overcame him because of the blood of the Lamb and because of the Word of their testimony, and they did not love their life even when faced with death." So we need to grow in our understanding of three keys from this passage that can help us.

The first key is to understand the "blood of the lamb." Jesus is the Lamb and His blood of protection covers us by faith, just like the blood placed on the doorposts of the Jewish people in Egypt protected them from the death angel. When you know you are covered by His blood, you know that you have a supernatural level of protection that will give you confidence while facing evil men or situations.

Second is the "Word of our testimony." In a court of law, we give testimony. We give confessions. Our testimony, our confession needs to be that "I can do all things through Christ who strengthens me" (**Philippians 4:13**). "Greater is He who is in me than he who is in the world" (**1 John 4:4**). We don't realize how powerful our words are and that the Bible even declares, "death and life are in the power of the tongue" (**Proverbs 18:21**). We need to speak out our faith and confidence in God and His Word.

And, of course, our words are more often than not a manifestation of our thoughts, what we think and believe about things. When we meditate on God's truths, then those truths will begin to feed our faith. We'll begin to think about ourselves, see ourselves, and speak about ourselves, and our circumstances the way God does. This is when we begin to overcome by the "word of our testimony." If what I believe about myself, and my future, and what I testify about myself, are in disagreement with God, I will not overcome in life. But when I think, believe and testify in agreement with God and His Word, powerful things will begin to happen, and I will begin to overcome the fear of man and intimidation.

You remember the ten spies and the people who didn't make it into the Promised Land we talked about above? Forty years later the people of Israel, led by Joshua and Caleb did enter and take the Promised Land. The land still had all the same nations as well as giants. But Israel still took the land. So it wasn't really the giants that kept the people out of the Promised Land the first time. It was their unbelief and their own words! They didn't believe they could do it and said so. Joshua and Caleb agreed with God, believed God and said so. They said, "We can do it! God said we could!" So our testimony (our words) is very powerful. The ten spies' testimony was, "We cannot do it." And therefore they did NOT overcome. Joshua and Caleb's testimony was, "We can do it!" And they did overcome by the Word of their testimony. They weren't intimidated by the giants or by the fear of man.

Take a minute to speak out loud some of these verses and declarations that I have mentioned above. Speak them out to yourself and the demonic fears and worries arrayed against you, just like David spoke to Goliath and Jesus spoke to the devil. You may think, "I sound and feel stupid saying these things out loud." Well, take your choice. When you speak out the negative testimonies and words that you have been saying in the past, you sound stupid to God! Did you ever think about that? He hears every word we speak just like He heard what the ten spies said. And those same negative, doubt-filled words actually feed the demons of fear and worry around you. They draw them and encourage them to keep coming around just like it does when you feed a stray dog or cat. But when you speak God's words they feed your faith. They strengthen your peace. Who do you want to feed?

Lastly, we can also overcome the fear of man by "not loving our lives even when faced with death" (**Revelation 12:11**). Of course, this refers in context to dying as a martyr. There is a freedom that comes when we are willing to die and become a sacrifice to God. Fear of those who might kill you is diminished or even eradicated completely. In Western Christianity, we don't think much about being willing to die for something, unless we join the armed forces, police, FBI, become a fireman, or something similar to these. Most Christians just don't think much at all about dying for something. Would you die for your spouse, children, or a friend? Our commit-ment is weakened because we don't think much about the true cost of being a disciple, which is death.

In fact, we are called every day to be a "living sacrifice" consecrated to God (**Romans 12:1,2**). Jesus told us to take up our cross and follow Him. Paul also said that he died daily (**1 Corinthians 15:31**). Before we will be able to die as a martyr, we must first be willing to die daily to our flesh, to selfishness, and pride. When we learn to take up our cross and essentially decide to die each morning as we get up out of bed, we'll find that fear doesn't have as strong a grip on us anymore. We'll begin to live and walk as Jesus did. He didn't love His life, even to death. He doesn't ask us to do something that He Himself wasn't also willing to do. But in asking us to die, He also gives us the power and the grace to do it. The amazing thing is that when we deny and die to the old, carnal flesh, there is resurrection power waiting to raise us up to new life, a life free from the fear of man. When you aren't afraid of someone who wants to kill you, then you are truly overcoming in life.

Fear of Sharing Your Faith With Others

"I'm just not an outgoing, people person."

Closely related to the fear of man we just looked at is the fear of sharing your faith with others. Jesus didn't say that only outgoing people had to share their faith. He commands that we all be a witness for Christ. So why are we afraid of sharing our faith? Of course, we need to be filled with the Holy Spirit. And if you aren't filled with the Spirit of God, you are out of the will of God and won't be filled with God's boldness.

But another reason is that sometimes we haven't been properly trained and mentored as a witness for Christ. Getting the proper training can be a big help, just like a soldiers training helps him to overcome many of the fears of combat. Also, ask yourself this question. Would I be willing to share my faith if someone gave me $1,000 for each person that I witnessed to for Christ? Of course, we need to be led by the Spirit when witnessing and not money, but the point is that He wants us to be sharing our faith often, even most days, or even every day! But most Christians *never* share their faith. But if you'd be willing to start sharing your faith for a thousand dollars, then that shows that your motivations are all messed up. Shouldn't we be sharing because of compassion for the lost? Aren't they going to hell? And also, Christ commanded us to share our faith. Anything less is disobedience. So we have to be working on this all the time.

But I want to talk about something else that contributes many times to the fear of sharing our faith with others. I think it's because we fear rejection? We fear that someone might laugh at us, mock us, or make fun of us, and we might not know how to respond. And so we'd feel embarrassed, humiliated, rejected.

When I was in high school, my favorite book was "*2001 Insults.*" I think that was the name of it. I read that book over and over and mastered the best insults and comebacks that I could find. High school sometimes was an intimidating place and if you didn't have the right ammunition to counter the constant cuts and insults of other people making fun of you, you were in trouble. I was afraid of being embarrassed, having people laugh at me, and feeling rejected.

But this is the point I want you to get. What is behind that fear? If you unmask the rejection, what you have is human pride. When we realize what we are really dealing with is our pride, we know who the real enemy is. We are proud and don't want to go through possibly embarrassing situations. We are afraid of being mocked and humiliated. It's pride. **Proverbs 16:5** tells us "Every one that is proud in heart is an abomination to the Lord." We have to admit that our problem is pride, and then repent of it. Then, we need to humble ourselves, and begin to do what we can do to share our faith. Begin to think about others, and not your own stinking pride. Humble yourself, and reach others who are headed to an eternal, devil's hell. Overcome fear with humility. Humble yourself and pray. Ask the Lord to help you. He will.

Evangelist James Robison was extremely shy when he was in high school. He would tell the teachers in his classes to just give him a zero if they wanted him to speak in class. He was just too shy and afraid. But then he got saved. He foster father was a pastor and helped him to learn to share his faith. But he still had struggles. So what did he do? He said that he would go up to a classmate in school and say, "Hey, I'm afraid about something." They would say, "What?" He would say, "I need to tell you something, but I'm scared." They would tell him to not be afraid and go ahead and tell them. Then pretty soon they would be afraid because they were feeling God's conviction of sin, and then praying to receive Christ! Since then the Lord has used him to lead millions of people to Christ.

The Unknown Fear

What is keeping you from doing what you need to do, or what you dream of doing?

For many people, there is a timidity, a hesitancy, or something indefinite that keeps them from making decisions, trying to get that job, trying something new, or following that dream in their heart. And so they stay stuck in a rut, unable to break through the fears that bind them and keep them from going into unchartered waters in life.

Fear of rejection, being laughed at, fear of failure or making a mistake are only a few of the fears that can cause us to freeze up instead of move forward. Fill in the blank to this statement. "I am afraid (of, that)…." You fill in the blank. Write it out in as much detail as you can. Doing this will help you to understand what you are up against. If nothing comes to mind, praise God. Forget about it. But if the Holy Spirit does reveal something to you, then share your struggles with your spouse, pastor, prayer partner, friend or small group leader. Studies have shown that most of us speak negatively to ourselves in our thoughts. So we need encouragement from those around us who will tell us that in Christ we can do it, and remind us of the promises of God as well.

Once you know clearly the fears or worries you're dealing with and have people around you that will help you, then you can begin to put together an action plan of steps that you need to take in order to do what you need to do. Remember, positive action will help to dispel fears and worries. Look around and find out about all the options that exist to help you to do what you want to do and overcome your fears. Fears usually grow in darkness and where there is the element of the unknown. When you learn more about what you are facing, and the options you have to deal with it, you will find hope rising in your heart.

And remember. God answers prayer. Ask God for ideas. Ask Him to help you to face your fears and give you the plan you need to be victorious. He promises that if we seek, we will find (**Matthew 7:7**).

Footnote:

1. Tibet Lonely Planet, 4th Edition, March 1999 – page 87

10

OVERCOMING COMMON FEARS OF THE FUTURE

Fear of Old Age and Uncertainty of the Future

"I've seen a heap of trouble in my life, and most of it never came to pass."
Mark Twain

As we grow older, we encounter new challenges, enemies and obstacles to our faith. One of them for many people is the fear of old age itself and the things sometimes associated with it. What we'll do for retirement, where we'll live, loss of a loved one, and the unknown are just some of the questions, fears or worries that people sometimes struggle with when growing old. For instance, my wife and I have raised our children on the mission field and so we didn't have a house in the United States. As I grew older, worry-filled thoughts would come to my mind at times concerning where we would live in our old age. The devil loves to come and say, "What are you gonna do about....?" If we don't know how to combat these kinds of fears and worries that may come against us, we'll be subject to demonic torment that God didn't intend for us to have. God's plan is for us to have peace and joy in every phase of life, including when we grow old.

What is the answer? Where do we turn? Again, our loving Heavenly Father has provided the answer in His Word and in our relationship with Him. Remember Jesus used the Word of God to combat the temptations that came against Him in **Matthew 4**. When we are tempted with fears related to old age, the Word of God is our weapon of choice in these attacks. Below are some Scriptures to help us be the over-comer that God has called us to be, even in the challenges of old age. We can face the future confidently, knowing that the Lord is our Helper, and He will meet our needs.

Concerning the example that I gave above, about worries of where we'd live when we got older because we didn't own a house, God led me to **Mark 10:28-30**.

> "Peter began to say to Him, "Behold, we have left everything and followed You." Jesus said, "Truly I say to you, there is no one who has left house or brothers or sisters or mother or father or children or farms, for My sake and for the gospel's sake, but that he will receive a hundred times as much now in the present age, houses and brothers and sisters and mothers and children and farms, along with persecutions; and in the age to come, eternal life."

Here the Lord promises to abundantly provide for missionaries, apostles, traveling ministers, and even regular Christians who may have left family, nice houses or moved somewhere in obedience to God in order to be where He wants them to be. You see, we are all called as Christians to live in the will of God, to live where He tells us to live, not just where we think would be good for our career or paycheck. What is God saying about it? That should be our first question. So whether you are an ordained minister or regular disciple of Jesus Christ, it is a sacrifice to leave loved ones for the sake of the Gospel. And it is a form of suffering to have to leave relatives, friends, and even sometimes children that we love for the sake of the gospel, to be where God wants us to be.

I lived in China for seventeen years. During part of that time, four of our children lived in or near the United States. Two of them were married, and we had grandchildren we didn't see very often. It was a price to pay. We wouldn't get to spend time with them for almost up to two years at a time. Thankfully we had technology and not only could talk with our children, their families, and our relatives, but sometimes we could also see each other through computer as well.

In the late 1800's and early 1900's, certain missionary sending boards had a rule that missionaries in China could only return home every nine years. They changed it to seven years after finding that most of their missionaries were dying before they got a chance to return home even once! When we were in Mexico (for five years), we had no telephone. So we usually couldn't talk with family back home for six months at a time. In our early days in Russia (1992, '93) we'd have to place an order for a phone call to the States one hour before the call. Then the operator would call us an hour later, tell us the call was connected, and then we could finally talk with family back home.

The point I am making is that the Lord sees the sacrifice. He knows and understands the suffering of separation that His children experience for the sake of the gospel. And God says that He will make it up to us. He is just.

And since we didn't have a house, the devil sometimes tried to take advantage of the situation and say, "Well, look at your situation now. You're getting older in years, and you don't have your own house. What are you gonna do?" Well, praise God, we have **Mark 10:29, 30** to use to rebuke those worry-filled thoughts, and build faith in our hearts to know that the Lord will meet all of our needs abundantly. He says that He will give us a hundred times as many houses, children, sisters, brothers, farms (businesses), and then mentions, "*along with persecutions*."

Does that mean God will give us literally a hundred houses? I don't know, but it sure means that He'll provide for you at least one house and abundantly meet your needs for shelter and housing. What I do know is that He will provide a house for any of His children who have made the commitment of **Mark 10:28-30**. Actually the Lord has provided about twenty houses for my family so far through the years as we have obeyed Him and gone where He told us to go. We've lived in Montana, Mexico, Russia and China. I didn't own any of the houses, but I didn't really need to own any of them either. He has provided.

One possible interpretation to this passage could be that when you add up the houses, brother, sisters, mothers, fathers, farms and businesses, it would add up to be at least one hundred. All of them together equal one hundred fold. But whatever the exact interpretation may be, God is a good God and will abundantly meet the needs of His children who have obeyed these verses.

The Bible says, "*The Lord is my Shepherd, I shall not lack.*" Whenever the devil was foolish enough to come around again with the old worn-out lie that I wouldn't have a nice house to live in when I'm old, I just pulled out **Mark 10:28-30** (Like a gun) and he would flee. Could I see it? Not at the time. But the Bible says that *we walk by faith, not by sight* (**2 Cor. 5:17**).

God has always provided for us and always will. Abraham was a prophet, God's servant, and friend. And yet Abraham lived in a tent! That was all he needed. He was like what we'd call a Bedouin today, a tent dweller. And yet he was one of the richest men on earth at the time. God blessed him because he obeyed the Lord and moved to Canaan land.

Sometimes, if we aren't careful, we begin to feel sorry for ourselves. Thoughts of self-pity will try to take control. We have to remind ourselves that it pays to serve God. Sometimes we might be tempted to think about the cost and sacrifice. But God is a just God. He will make it up to us for any price we have paid to serve Him and spread the gospel.

We need to be grateful and thankful for what we do have. We should not forget all He's done for us. Abraham didn't have a western toilet or an indoor bathroom. Jesus didn't either. Many of the places I go to in China have an outhouse for a bathroom. Some places just have a log over a hole. And yet the people are smiling and happy. We need to keep things in proper perspective. We need to be thankful. And we need to use the Word of God. Remember that Jesus is not only preparing a place for us in heaven, but **Mark 10:28-30** also says God provides for us in this "*present age*," as well. Some people push all the blessings and provisions of God off into the future "when we all get to heaven."

But God wants to help us and meet our needs abundantly here on earth as well.

Recently the Lord led us to move back to the United States and base our ministry here so that we could more effectively minister in not just one country, like China, but in many countries, as well as the United States. And amazingly, the Lord beautifully fulfilled **Mark 10:28-30** by giving us a house that is completely paid for! When we returned to the States we had nothing with which to buy a house. But glory to God, I'm here to tell you that God's Word is true, and He will fulfill it to those who trust in Him. He is a good Father. Amen!

Now here's a Scripture that David wrote and would speak out loud to himself to combat fears and worries concerning the days when his body grew old and his hair gray. "I have been young, and now am old; yet I have not seen the righteous forsaken, nor his seed begging bread" (**Psalm 37:25**).

David wrote this by inspiration and experience. This verse can also help us to know and affirm that the Lord will not forsake us in old age either. He'll continue to meet our daily needs. The Lord has told us that He would never leave us or forsake us. "*I WILL NEVER DESERT YOU, NOR WILL I EVER FORSAKE YOU*" (**Hebrews 13:5**). And He affirms it again here in **Psalm 37**. Thank God, if you are a child of God. Draw comfort from His promise and the testimony of David.

Psalm 92:12-15 is also an encouraging and faith-building passage that every Christian needs in their arsenal of spiritual weapons. We can use it in prayer and believe God for our future when our life becomes "full of days."

> "The righteous man will flourish like the palm tree, He will grow like a cedar in Lebanon.

> Planted in the house of the LORD, They will flourish in the courts of our God. They will still yield fruit in old age; They shall be full of sap and very green,
> To declare that the LORD is upright; He is my rock, and there is no unrighteousness in Him."

When we live a faithful life to the Lord, according to this verse we can count on and believe God that we will still yield useful fruit, and be a blessing in our old age. We can believe God to still be "*full of sap and very green*!" Someone may say, "Well, I know brother so-and-so, and he wasn't full of sap and green in old age." Well, I don't know what brother so-and-so was believing God for. Maybe he wasn't standing on this verse. Jesus Himself many times told the people that He ministered to, "*according to your faith*," and "*as you have believed*" be it done to you. If we don't believe that having faith in God's Word will make a difference, then our faith has been neutered and won't accomplish anything for us. Don't allow the devil to rob you of your confidence in God and His word. Jesus said that He came to give us life, and life more abundant. Abundant life is for every stage and age of life, not just for the young and youthful.

Remember what **Isaiah 40:28-31** tells us?

> "Do you not know? Have you not heard? The Everlasting God, the LORD, the Creator of the ends of the earth Does not become weary or tired. His understanding is inscrutable. He gives strength to the weary, And to him who lacks might He increases power. Though

> youths grow weary and tired, And vigorous young men stumble badly,
> Yet those who wait for the LORD Will gain new strength; They will mount up with wings like eagles, They will run and not get tired, They will walk and not become weary."

Strength is not just a physical phenomenon. Strength is also a spiritual force that we can receive and tap into by waiting on God and believing His Word and promises. Even young people's strength can run out, and they can also stumble and fall. But here the promise is that if we wait on the Lord, spend time in communion with Him, meditating on His Word, then that time will be converted into supernatural strength and power to carry us through, and even help us to fly over the circumstances and situations that we may face in old age.

I like **Genesis 50:24**. Joseph was about to die but before he did, he left some important words with his brothers and their families. He spoke truth and a promise to them. We should do the same. He prophesied and said, "I am about to die, but God will *surely* take care of you..." What an awesome and comforting word the Lord spoke through Joseph to them. He is speaking it to you and to me as well. We need to meditate on this word and believe it. When a father or a mother pass away or are about to pass away, we can take comfort from these words from the Lord. He will be with us, and He will take care of us. Hallelujah!

When these words become rooted in your mind and spirit, faith will rise in your heart and you will have peace at the thought of your parents, spiritual or physical, passing on to leave this earth and be with the Lord. This is why the Lord has left such verses to us. But the only way they can help us is if we meditate on them, believe them and speak them out. Say out loud, "Though my parents are about to die (Or have already died), God will surely take care of me." Then shout Hallelujah in the devil's face! Enjoy the peace and joy concerning the future that God intended for you to have.

And finally **Psalm 71:9-11** is a good passage to use in prayer to the Lord when looking at what seems like an uncertain future.

> "Do not cast me off in the time of old age;
> Do not forsake me when my strength fails.
> For my enemies have spoken against me;
> And those who watch for my life have consulted together, Saying, "God has forsaken him; Pursue and seize him, for there is no one to deliver."

The enemies he speaks of could be literal enemies, but they also could be the fears that we may face during the golden years. "My enemies have spoken against me." Fears and doubts may speak to our mind and oppose our hope and faith for the future. The devil may try to tell us that God has forsaken us, and there is no hope. But when we know the Lord, the future is always something we have to look forward to as well as the present.

And then the prayer continues in verse 18. "And even when I am old and gray, O God, do not forsake me, Until I declare Your strength to this generation, Your power to all who are to come." Any prayer we find in the Bible will, of course, be scriptural, and also a prayer that we can be confident is the will of God for us. It is a prayer that even in spite of old age, we'd be able to finish our race and the plan of God for each one of us. It is also a prayer that in our last days we could pass on to the next generation the assurance that God's grace is more than sufficient. His faithfulness will help us to overcome and bring glory to Him even through our death and passing on to heaven.

Fear of Future Illness

The future is as bright as the promises of God.
– William Carey

> "In those days Hezekiah **became mortally ill**. And Isaiah the prophet the son of Amoz came to him and said to him, "Thus says the LORD, 'Set your house in order, for you shall die and not live.'" Then he turned his face to the wall and prayed to the LORD, saying, "Remember now, O LORD, I beseech You, how I have walked before You in truth and with a whole heart and have done what is good in Your sight." And Hezekiah wept bitterly. Before Isaiah had gone out of the middle court, the Word of the LORD came to him, saying, "Return and say to Hezekiah the leader of My people, 'Thus says the LORD, the God of your father David, "I have heard your prayer, I have seen your tears; behold, I will heal you.
> On the third day you shall go up to the house of the LORD.
> "I will add fifteen years to your life, and I will deliver you and this city from the hand of the

> king of Assyria; and I will defend this city for My own sake and for My servant David's sake.'"'" (**2 Kings 20:1-6**)

> "While He was still speaking, they *came from the house of the synagogue official, saying, "Your daughter has died; why trouble the Teacher anymore?"
> But Jesus, overhearing what was being spoken, *said to the synagogue official, "**Do not be afraid any longer, only believe.**" (**Mark 5:35, 36**)

The fear of coming down with a dreaded disease is something that most of us have to deal with at one time or another in our lives. Many people live with a silent fear that Cancer, Alzheimer's or some other ominous-sounding illness is likely waiting for them in their future. But this is not the way God intended for us to live. Of course, fear attacks most people when they are told that they have an incurable disease. For some people, it could be the fear of a recurring condition or that past pain might come back upon them. Job even said, "What I feared has come upon me" (**Job 3:25**).

But whether you already have a sickness or not, if you give in to this kind of fear, it can open the door to a spirit of fear. And if you give in to it, it could possibly then also open a way for Satan to attack with illness. And, of course, when fighting an illness, fear will hinder the possibility of healing to a much greater degree, whether from medicine or divine healing from God. You cannot get healed as long as you are in fear. Far too many Christians have not been taught how to resist both fear as well as how to stand against sickness and disease. We have to learn to oppose it just like most people would resist the temptation to rob a bank or look with lust.

Many Christians think that we just have to accept sickness, and there's nothing we can do about it except go to the doctor. Frankly that is a deception from the devil, and it has tragically robbed too many people from even the possibility of receiving divine healing that God wanted to give them. But right now we're not dealing primarily with the subject of healing. We're dealing with the fear that often tries to grip people who have a serious illness. The devil will tell you, "*Well, your time is up. There is no cure. It's over for you now.*"

It's just like what the ten spies did after coming back from checking out the Promised Land for Moses in **Numbers 13**. They gave a bad report, the Bible says. The facts they told weren't bad in themselves. What was bad was that they said they couldn't take the Land that God had already told them He had given to them. They disagreed with what God had said! They let the size of the giants scare every bit of faith out of them. Now that is bad enough, but they didn't stop there. They made it worse by not keeping their mouths shut. They spread their fear, doubt, and unbelief and poisoned God's people with it, to the point that they lost all hope and heart (See **Numbers 13**). If you listen to the devil's negative, fear and doubt-filled thoughts, you will fall into fear and depression. And every filthy parasite of fear and worry will bore and wiggle its way into your mind.

Fear and worry are the twin sisters of unbelief. They join forces with sickness, or the thought of getting a dreaded disease, to try to gain entrance into your life and bind you. They want to keep you from growing in faith and getting healed.

Here are a few Scriptures to encourage and build your faith to know that God will protect us and deliver us from deadly diseases. God's Word will give us hope, and build our faith. But just like anything good and worth having in life, you have to fight for it. If you just roll over and give up, fear, hopelessness and worry will come in like a flood. But God's Word and the encouragement of His Spirit, as well as the encouragement of other believers, can lift us out of the mire of fear, and drive out the parasites of worry.

Take these scriptural pills three times a day, and starve out all doubts and fears.

> "*He who dwells in the shelter of the Most High*
> *Will abide in the shadow of the Almighty.*
> *I will say to the LORD, "My refuge and my fortress, My God, in whom I trust!"*
> ***For it is He who delivers you from the snare of the trapper And from the deadly pestilence.*" (Psalm 91:1-3)**

These verses encourage us that the Lord in whom we trust will deliver us from deadly diseases. Look at verses nine and ten.

> "*For you have made the LORD, my refuge,*
> *Even the Most High, your dwelling place.*
> *No evil will befall you,* ***Nor will any plague come near your tent.*" (Psalm 91:9,10)**

Verse ten tells us that no plague will come near us or our home. We need to get inoculated with **Psalm 91**. **Psalm 91** drives out fear and builds faith and security into our thoughts and spirits.

One of the main ways to combat fear is to give other people hope. Thank God for medical science, but sometimes there are things that it cannot do. It is limited. But our God is not limited. With God, there is always hope. His promises give us hope.

Don't let the devil use the old, worn out lie that healing and miracles all died out with the last apostles. Our God is the *same yesterday, today and forever* (**Hebrews 13:8**). His healing and miracle power is just as much alive and well today as it was in the New Testament. Jesus told us to pray, "*Your kingdom come, Your will be done, on earth as it is in heaven*" (**Matthew 6**). Did you catch that part, "…***as it is in heaven***"? There is no sickness in heaven. There is no pain in heaven. Sickness and pain are not part of God's will for the inhabitants of heaven, and, therefore, thank God, they aren't part of His will for His children on earth either.

Of course, there is so much more that can be said concerning divine healing. But it is beyond the scope of this book. Just remember, do not allow a spirit of the fear of sickness to get a grip in your mind and thoughts. Remember **Psalm 34** says, "I sought the LORD, and He answered me, and delivered me from <u>all</u> my fears." Praise God, He not only can do it, but wants to and will do it for us. But we have to do our part. Resist fear, and affirm faith in God and His promises.

FEAR OF DEATH

"O DEATH, WHERE IS YOUR VICTORY?
O DEATH, WHERE IS YOUR STING?"
1Corinthians 15:55

Fear of the grim reaper, death, is something that all mankind has to deal with. Of course, young people seldom take thought of death and dying. They see it but never feel that it is something that relates to them. But when confronted by the death of a young friend or classmate, even they are forced to deal with the stark reality that we are all going to die someday. They realize that even they shouldn't arrogantly whistle past the graveyard, as if they will never die. And, of course, anyone who hasn't believed in Jesus as his Lord and Savior should fear death. He is a fool if he doesn't. He lives in a delusion, thinking that he can jump from the airplane of death without the parachute of life, that only Jesus provides, to save him.

But when we come to know Jesus we are born again. For many, we are totally set free from the fear of death. Most Christians aren't so much afraid to die as they are to suffer before death, through torture or martyrdom, for example. God never intended for His children to suffer the fear of death for even one instant. He has provided the way for us to be at perfect peace about our future and also when we pass through the valley of death. But there are times when we all may be tempted to fear the experience of dying and that which is unknown to us. For whatever reason a Christian may begin to experience fear of death, thank God He has given us the answer and ability to overcome. We need not suffer the torment of fear of death. Again the Word of God comes to bring comfort, peace and the ability to live with joy in the face of death.

What are some of the things that can help us to overcome any fear of death? First of all, we need to remind ourselves and meditate on the promises of heaven and eternity with Christ. It's surprising, but many Christians don't know much about heaven. As a result, they don't have much of a solid foundation of faith and peace related to life after death. Without that solid foundation, it's hard to not be anxious and live above the fear of death. When our knowledge and faith in heaven are strong, and we are looking forward to going and seeing our Master and loved ones, then death can become just a door to go through to get to the other side. We won't fear it. Our focus is on the Lord.

We also need to feed on the verses that deal with the second coming of Christ and our being with Him for eternity. These passages help prepare us for the future hope that we have of, not only His coming for us, but also our spending eternity with Him as well. They get our minds off of death, and on the wonders we'll experience with Him.

Just as with other fears, when we get our minds off of ourselves and instead on others, we often experience freedom from worry and fear. We need to think about others who are going to die without Christ if we don't tell them. We need to get our mind on the task at hand of winning the world for Jesus and caring about those suffering around us. When we do this, the devil finds no fertile ground to plant his seeds of worry and woe.

And, of course, the main person we need to get our mind on is Jesus. **Isaiah 26:3** tells us "*Thou wilt keep him in perfect peace, whose mind is stayed on thee: because he trusteth in thee*" (KJV). When our mind is on Jesus, the Prince of Peace, and on His thoughts and words, there is no room for fear of death. He will never leave us or forsake us, and especially not at the moment of death.

One thought you may not have considered that can bring a measure of peace and comfort when we pass into eternity is knowing that angels will be there to escort us on the way. Look at **Luke 16:22**. "*And it came to pass, that the beggar died, and was carried by the angels into Abraham's bosom: the rich man also died,* *and was buried.*" Lazarus was carried by the angels to heaven. You too will have angels there to meet you. In fact, I believe at least one or more of them could be your guardian angel or angels who watched over you throughout your life from heaven but also on earth as well (**Matthew 18:10**). They may be the ones who escort you to glory. You won't be alone when you go to your heavenly home. Praise God!

Another comforting thought from the Bible that helps guide us through the gateway of death is knowing that there are brothers and sisters, loved ones and family who have gone on before us. And they are up in Heaven cheering us on, expecting us to stand strong through the trials we go through, including death. They, along with the saints mentioned in **Hebrews 11**, are included in the "*great cloud of witnesses*" spoken of in **Hebrews 12:1, 2**. It tell us, "Therefore, since we have so great a cloud of witnesses surrounding us, let us also lay aside every encumbrance and the sin which so easily entangles us, and let us run with endurance the race that is set before us, fixing our eyes on Jesus, the author and perfecter of faith, who for the joy set before Him endured the cross, despising the shame, and has sat down at the right hand of the throne of God."

Below are some passages of Scripture that get our thoughts pointed in the right direction to experience the peace and joy we have to look forward to, even though we have to pass through the veil of death. I start it off with the familiar verse from **Psalm 23:4**.

> "Even though I walk through the valley of the shadow of death, I fear no evil, for You are with me; Your rod and Your staff, they comfort me."

Untold millions of Christians have found comfort and peace knowing that the Lord is with them, helping them to pass *through* the valley. We can rejoice that we will make it through to the other side.

> **Hebrews 2:15** "And might FREE those who through fear of death were subject to slavery all their lives." (Capitalization emphasis mine.)

You can see so clearly through this verse in Hebrews that Jesus wants us to be free from fear, and has done what is necessary to free us from all fear. Take a look at Revelation.

> **Revelation 2:10** "Do not fear what you are about to suffer. Behold, the devil is about to cast some of you into prison, so that you will be tested, and you will have tribulation for ten days. Be faithful until death, and I will give you the crown of life."

Jesus is telling us to not fear suffering persecution or even death by martydom. We don't have to be afraid of it. God is with us and will give us the grace we need to go through whatever we may face, and even overcome it. If you are afraid, meditate on these verses, and know that the Lord will not allow you to go through anything without giving you the grace to do it.

> **1Thessalonians 4:13-18** – "But we do not want you to be uninformed, brethren, about those who are asleep, so that you will not grieve as do the rest who have no hope.

> 14 For if we believe that Jesus died and rose again, even so God will bring with Him those who have fallen asleep in Jesus.
>
> 15 For this we say to you by the word of the Lord, that we who are alive and remain until the coming of the Lord, will not precede those who have fallen asleep.
>
> 16 For the Lord Himself will descend from heaven with a shout, with the voice of *the* archangel and with the trumpet of God, and the dead in Christ will rise first.
>
> 17 Then we who are alive and remain will be caught up together with them in the clouds to meet the Lord in the air, and so we shall always be with the Lord.
>
> 18 Therefore comfort one another with these words."

If we feel anxious about the second coming of the Lord, and all that will take place at that time, God's Word can and will comfort us. You are His child. He is coming to take you to be with Him forever in heaven.

But some of you reading this may be feeling anxious about death because you aren't sure of your eternal salvation. You aren't 100% sure that if you died today you would go to heaven. Now is the time to make sure. Now is the time to repent of sin and pride. Now is the time to ask God to forgive you, and then proclaim with your own mouth that Jesus Christ is your Lord. I don't care if you're a church member. Just being a church member doesn't save you. I was a church member before I got saved. I also believed in God. But I had never truly and fully relinquished my rule over my life and turned it over to Jesus as my Lord and Master. Pray the prayer of salvation today. Turn your life over to Jesus. You will pass from death to life, and the fear of death will no longer have a foothold in your life. Then tell others of your decision. Write to me at gcbrooks777@yahoo.com or 104 Stonington Dr., Brandon, MS, 39047 and tell me of your decision. I will pray for you. And don't just stop there. Find and join a true, life-giving church that exalts Jesus Christ, being filled with the Holy Spirit, and the Word of God. Be baptized in the name of the Lord. Your new life in Christ, eternal life, drives out the fear of eternal death! Hallelujah!

11

"ALL THESE THINGS THE GENTILES EAGERLY SEEK..." (MATTHEW 6:32)

Fear of poverty and lack

> *"Do not worry then, saying, 'What will we eat?' or 'What will we drink?' or 'What will we wear for clothing?'*
> *"For the Gentiles eagerly seek all these things; for your heavenly Father knows that you need all these things.* (**Matthew 6:31, 32**)

For many people in the world, hunger, poverty and lack are daily challenges they face. The United Nations Food and Agriculture Organization estimates that there are 925 million malnourished people in the world today. Jesus said that famine and poverty would increase in the world as we get closer and closer to His second coming (**Matthew 24:7**). We as western Christians also face scary situations that could cause us to be fearful. The loss of a job, trouble finding a new job, lack of health or life insurance, the threat of the collapse of the national or world economy, losing all our retirement funds, or the company we work for declaring bankruptcy, the U.S. dollar losing all its value, are only a few of the serious problems that are happening or threatening to happen at any given time in our world today. If we aren't careful, this parasitic fear of poverty and lack will burrow its way into our spirit and thinking, sapping our joy, vitality, hope and faith. The only inoculation is taking a regular, full dose of our Heavenly Father's promises that speak of His caring for us and meeting our needs.

My wife and I were expecting our second baby and didn't know where the money was going to come from to make the final payment to the midwife who was going to help with the birth. We were praying and trusting the Lord to meet that need. I told my wife that somehow it would work out. One day when we were getting close to the due date I told her, "One thing is for sure. Whether we have the money or not, the baby is going to be born." Right at that time we received a check in the mail, almost a year late! It was from the telephone company where we had lived previously. They were refunding to us the deposit and other related funds they hadn't returned to us yet! The amount was enough to finish paying for the baby's birth. Praise God! God supplied our need from a source that we were not expecting at all. He is faithful. We just need to get to know Him and His promises much better.

Psalm 23:1 tells us, "The LORD is my shepherd, I shall not want (lack)." What a comforting and awesome promise. But as with most of God's promises, it is dependent on whether or not the Lord truly is our Shepherd and if we are following Him. It's a very nice thought, "the Lord is my Shepherd," but if you aren't really following Him, then experientially He isn't your Shepherd. If your way of living demonstrates that God is not really your Shepherd, then you need to repent very quickly and start following and obeying His Word. Only then can you rest in the promise that you "*shall not lack*" for food, clothing or any necessities.

Matthew 6:25-31 says that our Heavenly Father loves us and cares for us. One of the main reasons we worry, fear, and fret is because we don't really know Him very well. And because we don't know Him very well, we don't trust Him or think He'll do a very good job of taking care of us. But when we intimately know Our Heavenly Father through His Word and then, when we see His faithfulness experientially, we will have a peace that passes all understanding.

Matthew finishes the chapter saying what our responsibility is. In verse 33 he says that we must "seek first His kingdom and His righteousness, and all these things will be added to you." You can't claim everything being added to you unless you are fulfilling the condition of seeking and making Him first in your life. When we do that, God promises to meet our needs, and He will.

Finally, in **Matthew 6:34** the chapter ends telling us "not to worry about tomorrow; for tomorrow will care for itself. Each day has enough trouble of its own." This is not just good godly advice. It is a command of God. But you may be thinking, "How can I possibly not worry about tomorrow?" Well, get to know Your loving, caring, Heavenly Father through His Word. Then you can easily dispense with the parasites of worry and begin to enjoy His peace.

Your faith should end up being just like it was when you were a little child. If you were born in the West during my generation, most likely knowing where your next meal was going to come from, was not an issue. Your mom and dad were there.

They fed you and cared for you every day. Well, by meditating on God's Word, you'll come to know what kind of Heavenly Father He is. And when you pray and trust Him, you'll find out that He is faithful and true, even more than any earthly parent. You'll begin to have faith in Him just like a little child trusts his parents and has no doubt in the world that they will feed him, clothe him, and meet all his needs. The question is will we take the time to get to know Him?

Look at **Psalm 34:10**. "The young lions do lack and suffer hunger; But they who seek the LORD shall not be in want of any good thing." Either God's Word is true or it is not. If you believe it is true, then you'll be able to *fight the good fight of faith* (**1Tim.6:12**). And you'll rest in the knowledge that the Lord will meet your needs no matter how difficult the situation may be.

If you choose to meditate primarily on the alarming financial problems and possibilities facing the world today, you will probably develop a serious case of ulcers and spiritual parasitic fears and worries. Your faith in God and His promises will grow weaker and weaker while your faith in your doubts and fears will grow stronger and stronger. Whatever you feed is what will grow. Feed your faith and starve your doubts. And when you choose to dwell on God's promises that are faithful and true, all your fear and worries will melt away, and the parasites will be starved to death and forced out.

If you trust in the Lord, He can also even meet your needs through ravens just like He did for Elijah in **1 Kings 17:4**. He is *the same yesterday, today and forever* (**Hebrews 13:8**). What He did then, He can and will do now. This is not to say that there aren't real concerns and threats to world economic security that we don't have to consider. Of course, there are. But when you know that God is alive, He cares for you and still works miracles today, then you know that if you find yourself in such situations, it's no problem for God. He multiplies food, tells us where to put out our net so that we get a huge catch of fish, and also puts money in the fish's mouth that we are about to catch. All of this, He will do in order to meet our needs. The main thing is to make sure that we are *seeking first His kingdom and His righteousness.* Then He tells us that He will take care of all of our needs. Of course, if you aren't tithing and giving offerings to the church, missions and to whom God leads you to give, you aren't really seeking first His kingdom and righteousness with your money. But when you, the windows of heaven will open for you in amazing ways.

When we were missionaries in Russia, we gave birth to our fourth child, Ruth. She was born in the city of Izhevsk, in the republic of Udmurtia in 1993. The Russian economy had all but collapsed and it wasn't easy to find everyday necessities. For us, one of those necessities was diapers. We could have used cloth diapers but that would have made our lives and work, which were already very difficult, that much more stressful and fatigued. But there were no disposable diapers in Izhevsk either. Remember, Russia had been the Soviet Union for seventy years. Communism had yielded its typical consequences of poverty and lack.

The banks in Izhevsk also wouldn't give us dollars. In Moscow, we could use our credit card to write a check and get dollars. This actually worked out well for us because there *were* diapers in Moscow. So once a month I would travel on a twenty-one hour train-ride to Moscow to get money, and also diapers. I would buy just enough diapers to last us exactly one month. The train would arrive in Moscow early in the morning. I would go to the bank and get our money, then go buy the diapers and other things that we couldn't find in our city, and finally hop the night train back to Izhevsk.

After a year or so of this routine, the banks in Izhevsk finally started allowing us to get dollars! But what about the diapers? Amazingly, the month when the banks began to allow us to get dollars was also the very month when disposable diapers came on the market in our city! "And my God will supply all your needs according to His riches in glory in Christ Jesus" (**Philippians 4:19**). We serve a good and faithful Heavenly Father. Amen? Don't tell me that God won't answer prayer and meet our needs.

There are many other Scriptures that can also strengthen our faith and give us peace in the area of finances. **Philippians 4:19** says, "my God will supply all your needs according to His riches in glory in Christ Jesus." This verse is true. But just like all the rest of God's benefits, we must believe it in order to appropriate it for ourselves. All of these verses are like spiritual vitamins and medicine to strengthen our faith and spiritual immune system. But we have to take them, meditate on them and act on them in order to enjoy the benefits they offer.

Some people are going to suffer lack and be fearful of lack in the future because they have put their trust in man or a government instead of God to meet their needs. Everything that can be shaken in these last days will be shaken (**Heb.12:26-28**). If our trust is in our government and economy, then our faith is set up to be shaken, and shaken it will be. The only things that won't be shaken are those things that are built on the truth of the Word of God. God will allow everything that can be shaken to be shaken until our faith rests solely on Him and His Word.

Matthew 24 tells us that *lawlessness will increase* in the last days. I've heard Rick Joyner say on more than one occasion that one of the reasons this will happen is because of socialist governments and policies that have raised a population on entitlements and social welfare. Then, when the people finally realize that the government won't be able to meet their needs and be their god, they will take to the streets with mob violence and riots. We have seen this throughout history. Most recently we've seen this during Hurricane Katrina, and then the 2011 riots in London, Greece, and finally in the "Occupy" movements in various cities of the U.S. in recent years. Fear of lack will take hold of those who have trusted in man and governments to meet their needs but failed. Then their fears will morph into rage and lawlessness, just like Jesus predicted.

Jesus said that we must build our lives upon the rock (**Matthew 7:24-27**). Some people say, "My life is built upon the Rock. I believe in Jesus. I am a Christian." But although we know that Jesus is our Rock, this is not what He was teaching in that passage. Jesus was saying that being a *doer* of His Word was like a man who built his house upon the rock. There are many hearers in church, but not a lot of *doers*. It is only when we are doers that our lives will withstand the storms and crises of life. The storms of life come against us all, saved or unsaved, wise or foolish. But many Christians are being washed away by the storm or crisis. They either didn't know how to build their life on the Word in a certain area, or they were just simply not obeying what God's Word says about it. Sometimes a certain area of our life, finances, for instance, is shaken. Why? Because we didn't fully build that area upon the rock of His Word. We have to handle our finances the way God said in His Word. God will allow the financial problems so that we'll hopefully wake up and change the foundation upon which we've been building. When we've been building our lives on His principles and truths, things may be shaking around us, but our faith will stand strong, and we'll see that the Lord, He is God.

Another thing that we need to realize is that God's Word will not only help set us free from fear and worry, but His Spirit also will guide us. He will show us practical things to do to prepare for the calamities He warned us were coming upon the world. And, of course, being prepared is one of the things that we can do that will help to get rid of fear and worry. If we aren't responsible enough to prepare for future and common calamities by having savings, insurances, or the common storing up of food and supplies that even the government tells us we should have, then it could very easily open a door for fear and worry. Why? Because we aren't prepared when the crisis strikes, or looks like it's about to strike.

Joseph prepared for coming calamities. God showed Noah how to prepare. In many countries today, people still need to store up food and supplies for the winter like our ancestors used to have to do. If we are prepared when storms or calamities hit, we'll not only be prepared materially, but it will also help us to be prepared spiritually to fight fear. Then we'll be at peace when all around us is falling apart. We'll have something to share with those in need, and we'll also be able to tell them about Jesus and the peace that only He can give. We need to at least have the wisdom of an insect, an ant, which at the right time stores up for coming difficult times (**Proverbs 6:7, 8**). That thought leads us to our next point; the parasite called procrastination.

Parasitic Procrastination

"Don't put off until tomorrow what you could do day after tomorrow."
Mark Twain

Something you need to realize is that procrastination is also a culprit that opens the door to fear and worry sometimes. We must not procrastinate in making preparations for things that we know we should do, or things about which God has warned us. If we do, then we only have ourselves to blame for any fear and worry that finds an opening to get into our thinking. Noah prepared for the flood. He didn't put it off. The world didn't listen to his warnings to prepare and get right with God. As a result, the people went crazy with panic and fear as they watched the ark sail away in the waters of the flood. The Bible warns us in **Psalm 32:6** for "everyone who is godly to pray to God in a time when He may be found." Then it tells us why. For "surely in a flood of great waters they will not reach him." You have to seek God when you can. You have to prepare when you can. After the calamity has come, it's usually too late. That is what this verse tells us. Of course, preparing spiritually is the first area of our lives where we should be prepared every day.

I know that our Heavenly Father is merciful, and when we cry out to Him He will help us. But the fact is that there are times when God warns us about things and if we don't listen, we'll suffer the consequences. However, if we listen to the warnings like Joseph and Noah did, if we listen to His voice in us and His prophets in the church, we'll be ready. We'll be ready just like God wanted them to be ready. So realize that if you procrastinate and put off doing things that you know you should do to prepare for the future, it likely will be opening a door to fears that shouldn't be in your life. So heed the call of the Spirit of God, and you will be ready to reap a mighty harvest of souls, and bring peace to those in panic around you.

12

HOLD ON TO YOUR FREEDOM

"The price of freedom is eternal vigilance."

Spiritual things just like natural things can be lost, if we aren't careful. You may not be aware of this but it is still very true, nevertheless. I had made great gains and victories in my life over fear and worry. But I found that I had to guard it and maintain it if I wanted to continue to enjoy what the Lord had done. I found that fear and worry would try to come back. If I stayed strong in the Word, there was no problem at all. But if I began to neglect meditation in the Word, and especially the verses that ministered peace to me, then I found the attacks would begin to bother me again. Just like a fire has to be fed or it will go out, so it is with spiritual things. We can grow rusty and lose spiritual ground that we have gained if we aren't careful. We must continue to feed the fires of our spirit to stay in love with Jesus, and maintain the peace that comes through a close relationship with Him and His Word.

Revelation 2:25 says, "Nevertheless, what you have, hold fast until I come." A large number of Christians think that everything spiritual that happens in their lives is dependent on God alone. That is deception. The truth is, you and I have a part to play also, a very important part. We have a responsibility to fulfill if we are to experience the fullness of God's blessings in our lives. Here it tells us that we have to "hold fast." He doesn't say that God will do it for you. In fact, he is saying that if you don't do it, if you don't hold fast, then it won't get done. God will not do it for you. God will help us, and give us grace, but we have a part to play. And if we don't do our part it won't get done. It's just that simple. We have to hold on to the blessings of God or we will lose them. We have to hold on to the peace of God and victory over fear and worry, or it's possible that we will lose ground and have to gain it again. Of course, don't be afraid and worry about it. Just do your part. Fulfill your responsibility. Continue to meditate on the Scriptures and truths that helped you to get what you needed in the first place.

Luke 8:15 continues with this truth. "But the seed in the good soil, these are the ones who have heard the word in an honest and good heart, and hold it fast, and bear fruit with perseverance." Here we see again that we are told that we have to "hold fast" to the fruit we gain in life. In fact, every good and worthwhile thing in life has to be protected.

You may be thinking, "Why is it this way? Why do we need to 'hold it fast?' Why does it have to be protected? I thought if God did something then it would stay done." Well, of course, that is true. What God does stays done. But on the other hand, when it involves mankind, we have seen that there are other factors that are involved. Many of God's promises are conditional. They are contingent on man and how he responds and what he does. Jesus told many people, "Your faith has made you whole." He didn't say that His faith made them whole. He made it clear that the determining factor was what they themselves did and the part that they played.

Another very important factor we must realize is that we have an enemy who is intent on stealing and robbing from us everything that God has given and wants to give to us. Look at **Luke 8:5, 12**.

> 8:5 "The sower went out to sow his seed; and as he sowed, some fell beside the road, and it was trampled under foot and the birds of the air ate it up.
>
> 8:12 "Those beside the road are those who have heard; then the devil comes and takes away the word from their heart, so that they will not believe and be saved.

You see the activity of the devil is to come and "take away" what the Lord has sown and given. He doesn't want God's truths to take root in our hearts. The seed hadn't gone into the ground, or the heart of the person where it could be better protected.

John 10:10 describes for us very clearly the work of the devil. He is a thief. He steals. And if we become free through what Jesus Christ has done for us, the devil will come back and try to steal it from us again! He is like a hyena or a wolf. If they steal something and then it's taken away from them, they will then get other wolves or hyenas to help them get it back if they can. The devil will always try to take back ground that he has lost. It is one of his strategies that we must not be ignorant of. Look at **Matthew 12:43-45**.

> 12:43 "Now when the unclean spirit goes out of a man [When it is cast out.], it passes through waterless places seeking rest, and does not find it.
>
> 12:44 "Then it says, 'I will return to my house from which I came'; and when it comes, it finds it unoccupied, swept, and put in order.
>
> 12:45 "Then it goes and takes along with it seven other spirits more wicked than itself, and they go in and live there; and the last state of that man becomes worse than the first. That is the way it will also be with this evil generation."

Here we see the demonic strategy of the devil. When a demon has been cast out, he will seek to return, if he can. He comes back with other spirits, tries to get back in, and then get an even stronger hold than he had the first time. Sometimes he can get back in, sometimes not. Sometimes he can get back into the thinking of the person, but sometimes not.

How is he able to get back in? How can we stop this? The key is in verse 44. He finds his old house (person) "unoccupied, swept and put in order." What does this mean? It means the person was set free, but then didn't fill the house, his life, with the Holy Spirit. He didn't fill his life with the Word of God either. It was left "unoccupied." If we don't fill our hearts and minds with the Word of God, get filled with the Holy Spirit, and renew our minds (**Romans 12:1,2**), then that leaves a place for the enemy to attack and try to get back into. In order to hold onto the freedom and peace that we have gained in Jesus Christ, we must fill our lives with the Word of God.

Jesus said that we must "abide in Him and His Word abide in us" (**John 15:7**). **Colossians 3:16** says, "Let the Word of Christ dwell in you richly." You must realize that we are in spiritual warfare. You can't just treat the Word of God in a lackadaisical way and expect to overcome in life. You have to live in the Word and let it live in you. The way you let it live in you is to obey it. Obeying is exercising spiritual muscles. The Word of God is your daily spiritual food. If you don't eat physical food, your body will become weak. It is the same spiritually. If you neglect daily feeding and meditation on the Word of God, it is inevitable that you will become weak spiritually. Also if you don't exercise spiritually by obeying the Word, you will grow even weaker. So determine to be a faithful disciple of Jesus Christ and not allow the devil to take back what he stole from you in the first place.

Galatians 5:1 tells us, "It was for freedom that Christ set us free; therefore keep standing firm and do not be subject again to a yoke of slavery." Jesus wants us to be free from fear, free from worry. That is part of what He bought and paid for us on the cross. But there is a temptation to take our freedom for granted. When we do this, we are in danger of losing the spiritual freedom that we have gained.

Israel had basically taken the Promised Land through the leadership of Joshua. But in later years they went through a series of generations and kings where they lost their freedoms and then regained them, over and over again. We must learn from their mistakes and stay as close to the Lord as we possibly can. Only by living close to the Lord and staying full of His Word can we hope to maintain and keep the freedom that we have gained in Jesus Christ.

In **Hebrews 4:14** we are told, "Therefore, since we have a great high priest who has passed through the heavens, Jesus the Son of God, let us hold fast our confession." **Hebrews 10:23** similarly says, "Let us hold fast the confession of our hope without wavering, for He who promised is faithful." So another way that we keep the freedoms that we have gained in Christ is by confessing and declaring them vocally. In other words, we release our faith by speaking the truths of God's Word. I must say the same thing about myself that God says. Too many Christians negate God's Word and truth in their lives by disagreeing and speaking in contradiction to what God says. Many Christians without realizing it speak lies, doubt, unbelief, and defeat over their lives almost every day by speaking things that are in direct contradiction to God's holy Word. We should be saying, "I am more than a conqueror. Jesus has set me free from fear and worry. I am a believer, not a worrier. I believe in God. He is with me! I don't have a spirit of fear. I have a Spirit of power, love and a sound, peace-filled mind, a courage-filled mind, in Jesus' name!" These are the kinds of confessions that build faith on the truths of God's Holy Word.

You may say, "But I don't feel those things are true." If you live by your feelings, you will always be a defeated Christian. But if you live by faith in God's truth and confess God's truth, the good feelings that accompany faith in God's truth will surely come.

It has been said that the price for freedom is eternal vigilance. I believe that this is patently and absolutely true. We have to watch over and guard the freedom that we have gained in Jesus Christ. **Proverbs 4:23** says, "Watch over your heart with all diligence, for from it flow the springs of life." You see we have a responsibility before God to watch over our hearts and our thoughts. God will not do it for us. And if we don't do it, we'll lose it. The "springs of life" will begin to get clogged and they will shrink until our river runs dry. It's just that simple.

The second Congress of the United States voted that all coins should have an image of freedom on them so that we would never forget the cost of freedom and take it for granted. Now there isn't a single coin that has an image of freedom on it anymore. And guess what. We have lost more freedoms in the last few years than ever before. It is the same for us spiritually.

It's up to you and me, my friend. Let's pay the price of freedom. Lets keep guard over the precious things that God has given us through the sacrifice of Jesus Christ. Only then can we hope to fully fulfill God's purpose and plan for our lives. Only then can we hope to reach this world for Jesus Christ.

13

FAITH, OR FEAR OF PERSECUTION AND THE END TIMES

"When our faith in God is growing,
our fears and worries are going."
– Clay Brooks

Corrie Ten Boom is the amazing Dutch sister who, by the grace and power of God, survived a Nazi Concentration camp during World War II. She travelled the world preaching the gospel and wrote many books. She also wrote a letter in 1974 and told the story of meeting a Chinese church bishop. He explained to her, "*We have failed. We should have made the people strong for persecution, rather than telling them Jesus would come first. Tell the people how to be strong in times of persecution, how to stand when the tribulation comes, to stand and not faint.*" 1

Tragically, many Chinese Christians were told the Rapture, when Jesus comes back the second time to take His church-bride with Him, would come before the Tribulation or any persecution. Some of these were told and taught this by missionaries.

God have mercy on the missionary and pastor who doesn't prepare his people for the coming difficulties of the End Times we are living in, and which will grow even more difficult in the days ahead. In essence, these Chinese Christians were deceived, and, therefore, unprepared for what befell them.

In South Vietnam, before it fell to the Communists, native Christians were told the same thing. Both Chinese and Vietnamese Christians were left unprepared. China and South Vietnam fell into barbaric darkness. Christians were killed. Churches were closed. Some pastors and church leaders were thrown into prison for as much as twenty years or more.

Corrie was no stranger to persecution, tribulation, and suffering. She strongly said that those who teach that Christians won't go through the tribulation "*are the false teachers that Jesus was warning us to expect in the latter days*!" Shocking words from our highly respected sister who has already gone to be with Jesus. Nevertheless, they are words that should be taken to heart and seriously considered by the church today.

We need to realize something. If we are asleep, we have to wake up to what is already happening prophetically and to what is still to come. Sister Corrie continued in her letter, "*In America, the churches sing, 'Let the congregation escape the tribulation,' but in China and Africa* [North Korea, Cuba, and other countries also] *the tribulation has already arrived*." If they had been warned and told to expect the possibility of persecution and tribulation, they would have been ready and prepared for what was to come. To be sure, some could see what was coming, and tried to warn their flocks, but sadly most of the church was unprepared. As a result, many church leaders were unprepared for the government threats and pressures that were put on them. They were pressured and tortured to deny their faith and betray their Christian convictions. They weren't ready when they had to choose between deprivation and prison, or to deny Christ. If they had been prepared spiritually, their faith would have been stronger. They would have had more grace to overcome what was coming against them. But since they weren't prepared, anxiety, fear and ultimately terror gripped their hearts. They weren't ready for the spiritual and literal onslaught that came against them.

Some may be thinking, "Who are you to be criticizing those who, after suffering such intense persecution, betrayed fellow Christians and denied the Lord? Maybe they weren't ready, but you still haven't been through what they went through. Don't criticize." It's true. I haven't gone through that level of persecution for my faith. But sister Corrie did. And that doesn't change the fact that knowing and believing the truth will help us. Certainly believing a lie will not help. It will, on the contrary, hinder and hurt us. The Bible says, "You will know the truth and the truth will make you free (**John 8:32**)."

If we think that Jesus is going to come rapture us out of this world, when actually His plan is to help us overcome the world, we won't be prepared. That's a cinch. The devil will be laughing, and we'll be wondering what happened. **Revelation 12:11** says, "And they overcame him because of the blood of the Lamb and because of the word of their testimony, and they did not love their life even when faced with death." They overcame. They overcame fear. They overcame terror. They overcame government persecution and the antichrists that came against them. And that is what we are called to do as well, brothers and sisters. But in order to overcome we must prepare!

So what do we do? How do we prepare? **1 John 5:4** tells us what our calling and destiny is. It says, "This is the victory that helps us to overcome the world --- our faith." Lets look at the full verse (**1 John 5:4**). **"For whatever is born of God *overcomes the world*; and this is the victory that has overcome the world--our faith."** We could also say this verse another way to help us in our study here. "Whatever is born of God *overcomes fear*, and this is the victory that has *overcome fear—our faith*."

In order to overcome fears and worries about what the future and end times hold for us, we must be growing in faith and building stronger faith in God and His promises. We must be feeding and exercising our faith to make our spirit strong, just like we feed and exercise our bodies to make them strong.

You may be tempted to think right now, "Well, I've lived my Christian life so far, and my level of faith has served me pretty well. I don't need to exercise and feed my faith. I'm doing just fine." Don't be a fool. Those were the very kinds of thoughts that Jesus warned us about.

Psalm 112:7, 8 also give us insight into what we need to do. It tells us, "He will not fear evil tidings; his heart is steadfast, trusting in the Lord. His heart is upheld, he will not fear." When your heart is steadfast, trusting in the Lord, you'll be able to stand against and overcome fear and evil news that comes your way. Your heart will be strengthened, and you won't fear. That is what faith does for the human spirit and mind. So in order to be victorious over worry and fear of the future, it is vitally important to be growing in faith and strengthening our faith day by day. You also need to be knowledgeable about what is clear in Bible prophecy about the end times. The better you know and understand something, the less you are intimidated by it, and the less you are fearful of it.

Faith, in essence, is knowing God, and therefore trusting Him, His Word, and His promises. But faith is more than just a noun. It is also a verb (believe), and therefore learning to release and exercise my faith, albeit small, is vitally important. It's absolutely crucial.

God has given us in **Hebrews 11** a list of men and women of faith whose lives can encourage and inspire us to face fears with faith in God, and in the midst of terror-filled times see God work for us miracles of protection, provision, and victory for His glory. They should be examples, role models and heroes for us today. When we see their lives, they remind us that God is alive. He loves us and cares for us. And when we believe in Him and seek Him, He will miraculously watch over us and use us for His glory. Look at what **Hebrews 11:6-10** tells us about faith, as well as a couple of the heroes of faith that we should learn from today.

> 6 And without faith it is impossible to please Him, for he who comes to God must believe that He is and that He is a rewarder of those who seek Him.
>
> 7 By faith Noah, being warned by God about things not yet seen, in reverence prepared an ark for the salvation of his household, by which he condemned the world, and became an heir of the righteousness which is according to faith.
>
> 8 By faith Abraham, when he was called, obeyed by going out to a place which he was to receive for an inheritance; and he went out, not knowing where he was going.
>
> 9 By faith he lived as an alien in the land of promise, as in a foreign land, dwelling in tents

> with Isaac and Jacob, fellow heirs of the same promise;
>
> 10 for he was looking for the city which has foundations, whose architect and builder is God.

Here we see that it pleases God for us to trust Him and grow in faith. But it says that in order to please Him and grow in faith we must believe that He exists, but even more, believe that He rewards those who seek Him as their God and source to meet their needs.

I share about Noah later on in this chapter, so right now let's look at Abraham. He heard a word from the Lord. The Bible says that "faith comes from hearing, and hearing by the word of Christ" (**Romans 10:17**). He believed that word and therefore had faith. He showed that he had faith by acting on the Word of God. It took faith to go to a place he had never gone to before. It says that he didn't "know where he was going." He lived in that new land as an alien. God had given him a promise. He chose to believe the promise. We are also aliens in this world. It is not our home. God has sent us here as ambassadors to represent His kingdom and spread His domain throughout the earth. We need to see ourselves as Abraham did, and realize that the promises of the New Covenant are our promises just as much as the promises that God gave to Abraham. We are to work to prepare the way for Jesus' second coming. He is going to usher in a new kingdom and new age where He reigns for a thousand years.

Now a lot of people, Christians included, are afraid of the anti-Christian changes they are seeing in America, as well as what they've heard about Biblical end times, the Tribulation, the future and what it might hold. **Matthew 24** is a chapter that most Biblical scholars agree refers to a time that was coming soon upon New Testament believers. But it also has a second, prophetic meaning that speaks of events that will occur right before the return of Jesus. One of the first things that He says in this chapter is to, "See that you are not frightened." He also tells us, ahead of time, what things are going to be happening right before Jesus' return so that we'll know in advance.

Many people are afraid of the unknown. But we, as Christians, should not be afraid of the future because Jesus has already told us many things that will be happening so that we can prepare and be ready for whatever happens. We aren't in the dark like the rest of the world. But if we don't prepare ourselves spiritually, and if we don't study God's Word to know the things that it tells us to expect, then we'll be subject to the same types of fears of the future of which the world is afraid and terrified.

Of course, many Christians have been taught and believe that before anything bad happens Jesus will come and take all believers away. But actually that is a relatively new idea (pre-tribulation rapture) and interpretation of end time events. It is a fact of church history that most Christians have believed that the Church will go through at least some of the difficult times and events predicted before the return of Jesus. The problem is that if you think Jesus is going to come and rescue you from the "birth pangs" and the terrible time called the "great tribulation," then you won't prepare and be ready for any of it. Most western Christians readily accept and believe the teachings they hear about Jesus rescuing them in the Rapture. This is not just because they think it makes sense, but because they don't want to imagine the difficulties and hardships they might face if they had to actually go through at least some of those events.

But whatever your theology on the end times and tribulation is, just remember a few Bible examples. Noah was protected, but he still went through the flood. Lot was saved from wrath, but he and Abraham both were there to see and experience it from a distance. God didn't remove them from it. He protected them through it. Also consider the children of Israel in Egypt. God didn't take them out of the situation as His judgments were falling. But God did protect them from the judgments. One example is they had light in Goshen while Egypt was in complete darkness. All the firstborn children and animals died in Egypt, but none among the Israelites who used the blood to cover their doorways died.

Right now, we are looking at the possibility of the collapse of the world economy. We are seeing the Middle East erupt in chaotic upheaval, civil and national wars. Weather is growing more and more violent, erratic, and unpredictable. Each year we see weather records broken and shattered. We also hear many reliable, Christian prophetic voices telling of earthquakes, volcanic catastrophes, and cataclysmic events to come. Police officers are being murdered in unprecedented rates, just because they are white or just police officers. Bad cops are killing innocent people. ISIS is cutting off heads, burning people alive and crucifying Christians. How are Christians to respond to such news and predictions? Well, first of all, we must remember "God hasn't given us a spirit of fear" (**2 Tim.1:7**). The Holy Spirit that the Lord has given us is a Spirit of "power, love, and a sound mind." So if we are making decisions and operating out of worry or fear, then we aren't walking in the Spirit of God. Also, the Bible tells us that the Kingdom of God is "righteousness, peace and joy in the Holy Spirit" (**Romans 14:17**). If we aren't operating out of peace, then we aren't functioning in the kingdom of God. Instead, we're operating under the influence of the kingdom of darkness. The Bible says to "let the peace of Christ rule in your hearts" (**Colossians 3:15**). If we are maintaining God's peace and letting it rule in our hearts, the kingdom of God is reigning. When we start walking in worry or fear, we get out of God's kingdom, and start shaking.

People sometimes literally start shaking when they are afraid. God has told us in **Hebrews 12** that in these last days everything that can be shaken will be shaken. Then it says that we have received a kingdom which cannot be shaken, the kingdom of God. If we are walking and living in God's kingdom, we won't be shaking in fear. Jesus is called the Prince of Peace. When and where He is ruling there is perfect peace, no shaking in fear like a leaf on a tree.

So what do we do? We begin by filling our minds with God's thoughts and promises which bring peace and faith. As we do this, we will find that God's kingdom of peace will become more and more established in our hearts and minds. We won't shake with fear when we hear evil tidings. We'll know our God is still on the throne, and that He is still alive, is working miracles and answering prayers today. He will never leave us or forsake us! We won't just be giving lip service to these ideas. We'll know them and truly believe them deep in our hearts and spirits. We'll be full of God's truth, and there will be no room for the devil's lies, worries, and fearful thoughts in our minds.

When God's Word becomes strong in us, it becomes a stronghold of truth. Look at **Psalm 9:9**. "*The LORD also will be a stronghold for the oppressed, A stronghold in times of trouble.*" When you feel oppressed by worry and fear, the Lord Himself can become your stronghold, if you do your part. We must help build the stronghold of truth by meditating on God's truths and promises. This verse speaks of the "*times of trouble.*" The end times are certainly the worst times of trouble the world will ever know. Man will be reaping everything that has been sown, the good, and the bad.

But the point is that this promise says that the Lord will be to us, and become for us, a "*stronghold in times of trouble.*" He will be a stronghold to those of us who meditate on this verse long enough until we really believe it and take comfort in it.

Noah knew what it was like to be living in very scary and dangerous times. The Bible says that the wickedness of Noah's days was not just wicked, but *extremely* wicked (**Genesis 6:5**). It says that during those days, men didn't get a wicked or filthy thought every now and then or once or twice a day. It says that all of their thoughts were continually wicked and filthy.

It goes on in verse six to say that corruption was at its worst. It says the world didn't just have pockets of sin in certain areas on certain streets, but that the earth was absolutely filled with sin and violence. You couldn't find an inhabited place where the people weren't constantly thinking about perversion and violence. Spelled out that means there was constant sexual immorality and perversion going on everywhere, as well as murder, rape, robbery and assault and battery. Not just some people were involved in these sins, but almost every single person on the face of the earth was involved in these sins. There were only eight people, Noah, and his extended family, who weren't involved in these sins and wickedness. The only place you would have been safe was to be with Noah.

Jesus said the last days, the end times, would be just like the days of Noah and Lot. We are either living in these days or in the days building up to this, if you haven't already noticed it. Lot's city of Sodom was full of homosexuals. When I was young, you never heard of or saw anyone who was homosexual. Now they parade down the streets. We have openly homosexual congressmen and leaders. Our Supreme Court has voted and forced homosexual marriage on all 50 States.

Also violence, murder, and rape are filling the nations more and more. Riots, wars and rumors of wars break out without warning all the time. Corruption fills the governments, stock markets and businesses all over the world.

The increase of storms, floods, hurricanes, tornadoes, tsunamis and earthquakes is growing in number and intensity, and is happening in unusual places as well. So wake up and realize that we aren't waiting for the end times, we are already living in them right now (at least the Birthpangs), and Noah is crying out to us to listen and learn from his example.

The Bible says that Noah was a preacher of righteousness (**2 Peter 2:5**). Noah had to be one of the bravest, most courageous men ever to walk the face of the earth. In the face of such perversion and violence, he preached righteousness and judgment to come to the people of the earth. He faithfully warned them. Not only did his preaching warn them, but his actions and preparations did as well. But the people didn't understand what he said or what he was doing. They just went about their daily lives until the day that Noah entered the ark, and God shut the door.

The point I am leading to is that the days in which Noah was living were very dangerous and frightful days. But not only that, fearful judgments were soon coming on the world. Dreadful things were about to take place. So for Noah, not only the present but also the future held what many would perceive as fearful and ominous events. Of course, living in the terror-filled times of Noah, he probably was in a sense looking forward to God's righteous judgment coming on the earth. It wasn't because of the fearful things happening, but because of the ceaseless wickedness and sin that was around them all. The patience of God was amazing because He waited hundreds of years until the ark was finished before sending His judgment. But Noah wasn't afraid. So we want to learn from Noah so that we too can live fear-free in the midst of a crooked, perverse world.

I mentioned **Psalm 112:7, 8** above, stating that it is a good passage to look at when faced with a fearful future. These verses can help us understand the way many people feel about the biblical End Times. It says, speaking of a strong believer, "He will not fear evil tidings; His heart is steadfast, trusting in the Lord. His heart is upheld, he will not fear." This verse is describing someone who "will not fear evil tidings." He's not afraid of the future or End Times. Then in verse 8 he says again "*he* will not fear." Who is verse 8 talking about? Potentially, it is talking about believers who can have and experience God's promises fulfilled when they walk closely with the Lord. When you look at the preceding verses, you see it is talking about a righteous man who fears the Lord and delights greatly in His commandments.

First of all, a righteous man is one who lives by faith. He is growing in faith by meditating on God's Word, promises, and truth. He is also exercising or using his faith in the situations and trials of life that come his way. As a result, it says, "His heart is steadfast, trusting in the Lord." Your heart and mind don't just automatically end up that way when you become a Christian. You have to feed them proper spiritual food that will strengthen and build up your faith. You also have to meditate on the testimonies of God's Word, and even the testimonies of other Christians who have seen God's Word be proven true in their lives and experience. These are the things that will uphold your heart the way verse eight teaches.

Noah was this kind of a man. He wasn't afraid of "evil tidings," the previously-never-heard news that the earth was going to go through a total, catastrophic event, a worldwide flood of water. Now Noah certainly would have been tempted to be afraid of this happening. Nothing like this had ever happened before on the earth. It hadn't even ever rained before up to this point! The earth was just watered by dew and a mist in the mornings (**Genesis 2:6**). How in the world could Noah face such an ominous and fearful event that was coming? Why wasn't he afraid? It says that he was "trusting in the Lord." That is what makes all the difference in the world. He had the plan and Word of the Lord for what to do and how to prepare. His relationship with God and knowing the Word and plan of God gave him peace and purpose. We also can have the same thing. We have God's Word that tells us what to do and how to prepare not only spiritually, but in every other way as well. We also have the Holy Spirit, who lives within us and will guide us in knowing God's will and path. But you have to believe what God has said and trust in Him.

You also have to focus on the right things, or instead of overcoming, you'll be overcome. Do you remember Peter walking on the water? He was doing fine until when? He was doing fine until he took his eyes off of Jesus, the Living Word. He took his eyes off of the Word and began to focus on the wind, the waves, the storm and then the natural law that says people can't walk on the water. You have to focus on the truth of God's Word. Peter had two things that gave him faith to walk on the water. The first was that Jesus was walking on the water. It was possible. The second was Jesus' word "come." Both of these things are what gave Peter faith, as long as he was believing them, and then also acting on them.

So what does this have to do with Noah? Noah heard the Word of the Lord, focused on it and acted on it. How is it that Noah heard the Word of the Lord, but no one else did? Noah was a righteous man who walked with God. When you are seeking God, walking with God and listening to His Word, God will communicate His truth and guidance to you. But actually everybody else around Noah did hear the Word of the Lord. They just heard it through God's messenger, and rejected it, probably because he was a man.

Now I already mentioned **Psalm 9:9** above, which says that God is "a stronghold in time of trouble." God was a stronghold to Noah in the times of trouble before and during the flood. But there is something very important that you have to see and remember. Noah had to do his part and build the ark. We have to do our part and build a stronghold of truth and promises of God in our spirits and minds by meditating on, believing, and confessing God's word. God helped Noah and gave him strength and wisdom to build, but Noah had to *do* it. God also gives us strength and wisdom to do the things he calls us to do. But we have to do our part. We have to listen to His Word. Read His Word and meditate on His Word. Act on it. Remember, **James 5** says that the ***doer*** of the Word is the one who will be blessed, not just the hearer.

So if we learn from Noah and other biblical examples we can say like **Psalm 46:1-3**:

> God is our refuge and strength,
> A very present help in trouble.
> Therefore, we will not fear,
> Though the earth should change

And though the mountains slip
into the heart of the sea;
Though its waters roar and foam,
Though the mountains quake
at its swelling pride. Selah.

These verses could refer to mountains slipping into the heart of the sea because of volcanoes or earthquakes. Waters roaring, and foaming could refer to tsunamis. Of course, "mountains quaking" refers to earthquakes.

Here are a few other thoughts and Scriptures below that you can meditate on daily until they get down in your spirit. Through them your faith for the future can grow. We have to look at the Lord and regularly meditate on His promises if we expect to have peace in the days in which we live. You have to feed your faith just like you do your body.

First, you need to be careful about what is your primary and main news source. If your main source of news is from the world, then you will struggle with worry, fear, and anxiety. We must get our daily news from heaven. Let the Lord and His Word be your primary and daily news source. I'm not saying to never listen to or watch the news on TV or the Internet. Just don't make it your main source. Put more trust in God, His promises and His Word. Spend more time meditating on His promises and praying about the problems in the world from God's perspective and you'll find that you'll begin to live on a different, higher plane than the world around you. And, of course, the Holy Spirit will show us things to come and speak to us if we will learn to listen to Him and heed His voice and guidance. Here is a verse in Ezekiel that lets us know what will happen if the world's news is our main source. We'll groan and complain because our trust isn't in the Lord.

> <u>**Ezekiel 21:7**</u> - "And when they say to you, 'Why do you groan?' you shall say, 'Because of the news that is coming; and every heart will melt, all hands will be feeble, every spirit will faint and all knees will be weak as water."

Instead, we should be looking at God's headlines and promises like in the verse below.

> <u>**Psalm 33:18, 19**</u> "Behold, the eye of the LORD is on those who fear Him,
> On those who hope for His lovingkindness,
> To deliver their soul from death And to keep them alive in famine."

God has promised to keep us alive in food shortages and similar situations.

> <u>**Psalm 49:5**</u> "Why should I fear in days of adversity?"

This is a good question. It implies that we shouldn't be fearing and worrying. We should know our God and that He loves us and is watching over us to meet every need.

> <u>**Psalm 50:15**</u> "Call upon Me in the day of trouble; I shall rescue you, and you will honor Me."

Calling on the Lord honors Him. It proves we are looking to Him as the answer. And then the testimony that we have to share later will honor Him also.

These next two verses challenge the presence of fear and the lack of faith in any believer. If we will take the necessary steps to grow in faith, we will overcome when attacked by fear of the future.

> **Matthew 8:26** "He said to them, 'Why are you afraid, you men of little faith?'"
>
> **Mar 4:40** And He said to them, "Why are you afraid? Do you still have no faith?" "
>
> **Psalm 9:9** "The LORD also will be a stronghold for the oppressed, A stronghold in times of trouble."

We must believe and declare that the Lord is a stronghold in times of trouble. He's not just a 'hold,' but a '**strong**hold.' We must meditate on this until we believe it. Then we'll have peace when those around us are struggling and washing away in the floods of fear.

Footnotes:

1. "When Jesus Returns," by David Pawson. Page 199.
   http://endtimepilgrim.org/corrie.htm
   "Tramp for the Lord," by Corrie Ten Boom, pages 116, 117,
   http://filesfromtoni.blogspot.com/2010/07/corrie-ten-boom-warns-against-pre.html

14

FEARING DOOMSDAY OR PREPARING THE WAY FOR THE COMING OF THE LORD?

Ms. Brazile, New Orleans, Louisiana, after Hurricane Katrina: "*We thought the government would come in and help us. I mean, what has scared the living Jesus out of everybody is that they let us suffer. They let us die.*"

Recently there was a TV program called "Doomsday Preppers." It's about people who are preparing for some kind of "doomsday" that they see coming. It could be an economic meltdown, catastrophic terrorist attack, coronal mass ejection, nuclear EMP bomb, international pandemic, or even some people who believe in a zombie apocalypse. For those who don't know Jesus and refuse His offer of salvation, what is awaiting them is a doomsday. But a better, more accurate description would be to call it *judgment day*. And that is what these people should really fear and be concerned about. Standing naked before God on the judgment day of all judgment days is what really should sober people and be on their minds more than some catastrophes or calamities that are coming to the earth in these last days.

But actually, to those of us who know Jesus, our greatest and most wonderful days are ahead. "How so?" you say. Even though the future will not be easy, those days can and should still be our best and greatest because the Lord will pour out greater power and glory on us as well. They will be days filled with harvest of souls, power, miracles, signs and wonders.

Whatever you may think about the TV program, there is at least one important lesson to be learned from it. That lesson is that one of the main ways we overcome our fears of the future is by taking practical measures to prepare. When we make preparations, especially preparations that we as Christians feel God has led us to make, we begin to feel more confident and ready to face whatever may come our way. That is the blessing of wisdom, the wisdom of preparation. Of course, there are spiritual preparations as well as practical preparations that we must take. In fact, the spiritual preparations are the most important, especially when planning for harvest of souls.

First of all, I want to remind you again that one of the things that Jesus said over and over when speaking of the end times was, "fear not." We should not make any decisions based on fear, but on the leading of the Lord. Back during the Y2K (Year 2000) scare, some Christians sold everything they had, moved to a remote location and bought food and guns in preparation for the disintegration of society. My pastor at that time, Rod Aguillard, said that in Southeast Louisiana we would do okay during Y2K. He said that we had enough road kill to keep everybody fed until it blew over.

During that time, prophecy and end-time teachers were also on the bandwagon, warning people of possibly the end of the world, and the coming of the Lord. Then, when nothing happened, everyone found out that there had been a big scare over nothing. All the predictions were wrong. So first of all we need to seek the Lord, calm ourselves down, and make sure that we are hearing from God, and not some spirit of fear speaking through someone, Christian or not. Then we can make the calm preparations (if any) that the Lord leads us to make, just like Noah did for the flood.

One of the fearful, future, planet Earth possibilities (and which is now a very high probability) is a worldwide, incurable pandemic. I'm referring to something like the Bubonic Plague, Swine Flu, Bird Flu, SARS, AIDS or any other incurable virus or plague that breaks out. And, interestingly enough, my family and I have some personal experience in this area.

In 2003, we were living in China when the dreaded SARS virus broke out. SARS is an incurable and deadly flu type virus, and therefore invokes uncontrolled fear in the masses. Chinese universities sent many foreign teachers home. They closed down villages, neighborhoods, and you couldn't go into many public buildings without first having your temperature checked. You had to have an ID to get back into your own apartment complex.

I took my wife out to eat for our anniversary during those days. We went to a local Sheraton Hotel, which is normally filled with foreigners, as well as Chinese. After we sat down to order and eat, we suddenly realized that we were the only guests in the entire hotel! That's right. We were the only ones. There were no customers, travelers or tourists at all. It was an extremely eerie feeling. Nobody was traveling to China. People were fearful of the spread of SARS.

Not long after our Sheraton experience, we went out to eat at another restaurant where we often ate with groups. Upon arrival, we were somewhat surprised to see that there were only a few policemen in the whole restaurant. No one else was there. Normally the place was full. Strangely they escorted us to a separate room although the main dining area was practically empty. Then, even more strangely, after we had been looking at our menus for a minute or so, the waitresses returned and told us that we would have to leave. "What? Why?" No explanation was given. They just apologized and told us they couldn't serve us. I believe what happened is the policemen told them to have us go. It seems they were afraid we might give them SARS, although the disease itself began in southern China's Guangdong Province.

We had American friends who were teachers at a University but weren't required to return home to the States during the outbreak. However, they still had to get special permission to leave the college campus to come to our Sunday worship service. They were only allowed to leave to buy groceries on a limited basis, and even that was only when a university vehicle could take them. Students weren't allowed to leave their respective campuses. If they were caught outside the campus, they wouldn't be allowed to return, or they even could be kicked out of school.

Everywhere, people were going around wearing surgical masks. It was a very strange and bizarre time. Many of these things were logical and normal precautions to try to stop the spread of the disease. Quarantine is a normal strategy to try to contain diseases. But the point is that all this abnormal behavior set everyone on edge. People were afraid. They were mainly afraid because they were caught completely unaware and off guard. They had no idea that such a thing was about to happen. And often that is how fear can grip us. It catches us by surprise.

Many people, including the US government agencies, have been warning citizens for years to prepare in case of an outbreak of an incurable virus or some other plague. Most people make almost no preparation, or absolutely no preparation at all. And so when it happens they are almost totally gripped by fear and panic.

Even if they had just taken the time to learn a little about such things and make a few basic, or small preparations, it wouldn't have caught them so off guard and knocked them off their feet. And they wouldn't have experienced the degree of shock that those who are totally unprepared feel when sudden outbreaks happen.

There is one other factor that is very important for us to remember when thinking about catastrophes and such things as outbreaks, food poisoning, and pandemics. You can't count on the government to warn you and take care of you in such situations. You and I have to be responsible for our own lives and make the necessary preparations for these coming catastrophes. And make no mistake! They are coming. It's not a question of "if" but "when." This is what the leading experts are telling us. We need to hear the voice of the Lord and be led by the Spirit of God. We should mobilize our churches and families to be ready to not only take care of our own, but also to help those suffering around us.

The not-surprising fact is that the Chinese government withheld and hid the information about the rapid spread of the highly contagious and lethal SARS virus from the public until a Chinese doctor fearlessly began speaking out! Thankfully, in America it seems that we are warned in advance of such things. But sadly, even here in the United States, politics often enters into dealing with contagious diseases, like we have seen in the cases of Ebola and AIDS. You and I must not count on the government to take care of us. We have to learn that we have to take responsibility for ourselves and take care of ourselves. If the government helps, then thank God. But if they don't help, and you didn't prepare, you will be caught in a very serious situation with no time to respond. Remember how bad the government response was after Hurricane Katrina, and how long it took them to get aid to the Superdome? A Ms. Brazile, of New Orleans, LA, was interviewed by NPR after Hurricane Katrina. She said, "We thought the government would come in and help us. I mean, what has scared the living Jesus out of everybody is that they let us suffer." 1 My Friends, put your faith in God, not in the government, or you might end up with the same response as this woman. And by the way, if you know the Lord and His Word, nothing is going to "scare the living Jesus out" of you. You will know that He will never leave you and never forsake you. Amen! Maybe the government will leave and forsake you, but Jesus never will. Hallelujah!

Again I repeat, we must meditate on God's Word, promises, and truths. We need to be listening to and hearing the voice of the Holy Spirit. Only the Lord, the Prince of Peace can give us peace in an increasingly chaotic world. **Psalm 33:18,19** is a good reminder to calm an alarmed and fearful heart....if we'll believe it.

> Behold, the eye of the LORD is
> on those who fear Him,
> On those who hope for His lovingkindness,
> To deliver their soul from death
> And to keep them alive in famine.

If we trust in Him, God is the One, Who will deliver our soul from death and keep us alive in fearful times. **Psalm 91** tells us of God's protection from disease and danger for those who "dwell in the shelter of the Most High" and "abide in the shadow of the Almighty." But we have to meditate on it until we fully embrace these truths and believe them in our hearts in order for them to work for us. All Christians should memorize this Psalm and have it in their spiritual weapons arsenal in order to "fight the good fight of faith" (**1 Timothy 6:12**).

> "He who dwells in the shelter of the Most High
> Will abide in the shadow of the Almighty.
> I will say to the LORD, "My refuge and my fortress, My God, in whom I trust!"
> For it is He who delivers you from the snare of the trapper And from the deadly pestilence.
> He will cover you with His pinions, And under His wings you may seek refuge; His faithfulness is a shield and bulwark.
> You will not be afraid of the terror by night,
> Or of the arrow that flies by day;
> Of the pestilence that stalks in darkness, Or of the destruction that lays waste at noon.
> A thousand may fall at your side And ten thousand at your right hand, *But* it shall not approach you." - **Psalm 91:1-7**

1 Peter 4:7, 8 also tells us how true spiritual "doomsday preppers" should prepare:

> "The end of all things is near; therefore, be of sound judgment and sober *spirit* for the purpose of prayer.
> Above all, keep fervent in your love for one another, because love covers a multitude of sins."

We need to be of sound judgment. I just read recently how a family in Utah was found dead in their home. They had all committed suicide, fearing doomsday was about to happen anytime. Only God's Word can give us "sound judgment" and clear thinking.

Increase in prayer is also something Peter mentioned here that we need to be doing when we see "the end of all things" drawing near. We are reminded of the admonition, "Draw near to God and He will draw near to you" (**James 4:8**). But he also says to be "of sober spirit" for the purpose of prayer. This implies that the reason many Christians aren't praying much is because they aren't sober. They are "under the influence" of drunken, demonic spirits, that lead us to join the world and live only for our own selfish pleasures. We need to slap ourselves, look around and sober up. At the time when we should be the soberest and awake, we are too often eating, drinking, and living for pleasure like the rest of the world. No wonder we are caught off guard and filled with fear when alarming things begin to happen.

Something else that we should remember is that we should be rejoicing that wickedness in the world is coming to an end when Jesus returns. Murders, rapes, pedophilia, child abuse, pornography, adultery and every other wicked sin that has filled this world will come to a thunderous end, in Jesus' name. We should be excited and expectant, looking for His return and the end of evil. I'm sure Noah was feeling this way in his day.

When looking at what the Bible tells us is coming, we need to realize that we are not just headed for the end of the world, but rather for a new beginning. Yes, there will be a process of doing away with the old world. But the main truth we need to focus on is that there is going to be a new beginning in which Jesus will be King. So don't focus on the "Antichrist," or the "Great Tribulation," and the negative things that will be happening. Know about them, and prepare for them as the Lord leads, but don't focus on them.

Two of the main words in the book of Revelation are 'overcome' and 'overcomer.' We are called to be overcomers of not only the flesh and carnal mind, but also of the world and difficult times that Paul and others talked about in relation to the end times. In **Revelation 12** it describes believers who would overcome. How would they overcome? It says that they overcame the devil by the blood of the Lamb, the word of their testimony (confession, declaration), and they didn't fear for their lives, even when threatened with death. How can we grow to be this kind of overcomer?

First of all, we must get a proper perspective concerning difficulties and tribulations. The Bible tells us in **Acts 14:22** that "Through many tribulations we must enter the kingdom." This is true for us as individuals, and it is also true for the whole world as well. The kingdom of God will be fully established as the world goes through these end time events and tribulations. As for Christians, if we don't already have this perspective, we must begin to see every trial, and every tribulation, as a way for the kingdom of God to be more fully established in our lives. The greater the trial or battle, the greater the victory can be, and the more that God's kingdom can be established in us. But we have to respond in the right way. The Great Tribulation that we see in Matthew 24 will be our greatest opportunity for more of the kingdom of God to be established in our lives. We should not be afraid of it.

Now, someone may ask, "What is the Kingdom of God? What does that mean in a practical way?" Those are very good questions. **Romans 14:17** tells us "the kingdom of God is not eating and drinking, but righteousness and peace and joy in the Holy Spirit." So if you want peace and joy in the midst of problems, trials and tribulations, then you need to begin to see your problems as opportunities for the kingdom of God to grow in your life. If you are losing your faith, peace, and joy because of problems and trials, then you aren't allowing the kingdom to grow in you. You aren't walking in the kingdom the way you should.

In order to be victorious in daily life, and in what is coming as well, we must learn to follow James' instruction to "consider it all joy, my brethren, when you encounter various trials" **(James 1:2)**. We should learn to not look at irritations, aggravations, and problems as something over which we lose our peace or joy. It may sound absurd, but what we need to do is rejoice in our trials. We need to praise God for another opportunity to see that His Word is true, and His promises can help us overcome in any situation. If we respond to our problems correctly, we can have more of God's kingdom of faith, peace, and joy growing in our lives to such a degree until we are overcomers in all things.

Some people just want God to come and rescue them and take all their problems away. We can stop some problems by using our "commanding authority" in Jesus' name. But other problems are not that way. We must realize that the Bible says that as long as we are in this world we will "have tribulation"

(**John 16:33**). In fact, this is what is going to increase more and more in the days ahead. But He tells us to "not fear" these tribulations or the "great tribulation." He has overcome, and therefore we have the potential in us to overcome in life as well. How do we overcome? By just waiting around for Jesus to come rescue us? No. By believing that "greater is He who is in us, than He who is in the world" (**1John 4:4**). We overcome by learning to consider it "all joy," when faced with problems and a fearful future.

How can we have joy when we see suffering, tribulation, and problems increasing around us? By having learned to keep our eyes on Jesus. We can have joy knowing that He is returning, and that He is going to bring in a new, healed, and restored world. No, it's not a New Age new world. Jesus described the new, godly world coming thousands of years before the recent New Age Movement began.

When David faced Goliath, the Bible says that he ran *toward* the giant. He ran *toward* the battle. We aren't supposed to be trying to run from our problems or tribulations. That's not to say that there aren't times when wisdom would guide us to avoid a situation. But we need to be sure it is wisdom and not fear that is guiding us. A true warrior will run TO the battle! David had learned through previous battles with bears and lions to trust in God and run to the battle. We must do the same with our smaller battles in life so that we'll be ready when the bigger battles come, as surely they will. When we are trained for war and know our spiritual weapons and the authority we have in Jesus Christ, we won't be afraid to face giants, tribulations, or antichrists. We'll rise up and face them by faith, in Jesus' name. We may be tempted to fear and run, but we won't.

The Bible has told us that everything that can be shaken will be shaken (**Hebrews 12:26-28**). In fact, right now, this is exactly what is happening in the world. Economies, governments, jobs, etc…are all being shaken. And if our trust is in anything more than God, we will also be shaken. Why? So that we will build our lives on the only solid foundation, which is trust in God and His Word.

Jesus told the parable about the wise and foolish builders in **Matthew 7:24-28**. One built his house (life) on the sand, and the other built his house (life) on the rock. The rain, floods, and winds came against both of the houses, but only one was still standing after the storm had passed. It was the wise man's house, built on the rock. It was unshakable. Why? How? Jesus said in verse 24, "Therefore everyone who hears these words of Mine and acts on them..." Notice, hearing His words is not enough. Many people hear the words and teachings of Jesus. But if that is all they do, it won't really benefit them. It won't help them through the storms and crises of life. You must act on Jesus' words. You must do what He says.

When things start shaking, we may start feeling fear and worry. That shows us that we haven't solidly built our lives on thinking God's thoughts and being *doers* of the Words of Jesus. You can't just say, "I believe in Jesus. I'm built on the rock." No, not really. According to Jesus and the context of this parable, being built on the rock means to be a *doer* of the Word of God. If you aren't doing what Jesus taught, then when trouble comes, you will be shaken. That's why many Christians shake and some fall apart when the storms and crises of life come. They aren't doers in every area of their lives. If an area starts shaking in fear or worry, recognize that it isn't built on God's Word. Begin changing your actions. Begin changing the way you talk. Begin to believe in the Word and promises of God. Start to build on the true rock and then true peace will begin to return.

So take inventory. Evaluate and see which areas of your life have no peace, or where you really aren't a doer of the Word of God. Begin to build your life on the rock by being a doer and you'll be able to not only weather the storms, but even come out on top, victorious in them.

In fact, the truth about the matter is that we are the ones who should be causing things to shake. We should be shaking things up instead of us being the ones shaking. Shake things up with love. Shake things up with truth. Shake things up by praising and worshiping God. Shake things up by sharing the gospel, and casting out demons. All of these things are like Holy Ghost Gospel bombs that go off, and shake things up and destroy the works of the devil.

One other secret to help us overcome and face the future with faith instead of fear is found in an ancient Old Testament feast known as the Passover. Found within this important Hebrew feast is a vital faith practice we need to understand and be doing to prepare spiritually for now and the future. In the book of Exodus, the children of Israel were about to leave Egypt. Pharaoh was about to relinquish his grip on the children of Israel, but God was going to judge the Egyptians with one last judgment. God said a death angel was going to pass through Egypt and kill all the first-born children of man and beast. If you had been a part of that first Passover, the only way to save and protect your family would have been to follow God's instructions and put lamb's blood over and around the door to your house.

Another important point I want you to see is that death would come not only on the Egyptians, but also on the children of Israel as well. Hebrew and Egyptian alike had to use the lamb's blood on the doorpost if they wanted to be protected. So whether you were Hebrew or Egyptian, you had to have the blood on your house or the firstborn would die. So what does that mean to us in a practical sense today? We also must, by faith, claim and spiritually put the blood over our household and property each day. Now, we don't have to go out and kill a lamb and put its blood on our doorpost. Jesus is the true Lamb of God. His blood has already washed us clean from our sin. But there is much more power in the blood of Jesus than only cleansing of sin, as important as that is. We can and should claim the protection of the blood of the Lamb of God, Jesus Christ covering and protecting us from danger, harm, and other types of calamities. His blood can protect from theft, wrecks, from dangerous storms and even violent attacks. But we have a part to play in this. It won't just fall into our lap like a ripe apple. We have to claim it by faith. You and I have to speak it out with our mouths and say, "Lord, in Jesus' name, I claim your blood of protection over my family and my property. Destruction must pass over me without harming or hurting, in Jesus' name."

Maybe this is the first time you have ever heard that Christians can and should be doing this kind of thing. It may seem strange to you because you haven't been taught this biblical practice before. There certainly is biblical foundation in the Word of God for this practice, and it has brought comfort and protection not only to me but also to millions of Christians around the world. The practices and examples of the Old Testament are types and symbols that are fulfilled in the New Testament and lived out now by believers in Jesus Christ. We can take advantage of everything provided for us through Jesus and His sacrifice. And certainly protection is something that the Lord provides for us, His children. Maybe you haven't been experiencing His protection because you haven't been claiming it. You haven't been praying about it and claiming by faith His blood over your life and property. We have a part to play in these things. We have to, by faith, apply the blood over us each day.

But don't just try it. You have to pray about it, and meditate on the Word and truth of God until it gets into your spirit, and you know that it's true and believe it. Then when you speak it out and claim it, it will work for you. Of course, you still have to listen to and be led by the Holy Spirit. If you aren't being led by the Spirit of God you may be doing something He doesn't want you to do or be somewhere you shouldn't be. In that case, you can't expect God's protection to be on your life. You can only claim God's protection when you are in the will of God.

So take advantage of all that is provided for you by the blood and sacrifice of Jesus. Live in the power and protection of the blood of Jesus, the Passover Lamb. This will add another protective layer of peace in your life to help you overcome now and in the future.

In the midst of the catastrophes that the Word of God tells us will be happening during the end times right before Jesus returns, we must also remember that **we have a job to do**. We are supposed to be preparing the way for the coming of the Lord. He's not only physically coming back to earth, but also coming by His Holy Spirit in revival and harvest. But we have to do our part and prepare the way spiritually for what God wants to do. The Lord tells us to arise in the midst of the darkness and let our lights shine for the glory of God! Jesus said that one of the ways we let our lights shine is to do good works (**Matthew 5**).

One of the ways that churches need to prepare and shine their lights is to have emergency response teams that can move out in a moment's notice to earthquake, flood, and tornado hit areas. We can arrive with needed food, water, and shelter, letting the people know that Jesus is the answer, and God loves and God cares. Yes, arise in prayer! Yes, arise in obedience to preach the gospel! Yes, arise in obedience to go into all the world to those who have never heard! But remember that Joseph and Noah prepared in practical ways to help people and even animals during catastrophes. Noah was preparing for a flood. Joseph was preparing for a famine. Jesus said that earthquakes, floods and catastrophes would be increasing more and more just like birth pangs of a woman in labor. If we aren't ready, we will have no excuse when we stand before the Lord.

Isaiah prophesied not only of the time before the first coming of the Lord, but also of our day. Who will hear what the Spirit says to the churches?

> "**Arise, shine**; for your light has come, And the glory of the LORD has risen upon you.
> "For behold, darkness will cover the earth And deep darkness the peoples; But the LORD will rise upon you And His glory will appear upon you.
> "Nations will come to your light, And kings to the brightness of your rising. – (**Isaiah 60:1-3**)

You may feel and think, "Well, I don't see any light or glory." Where is your faith, my brother, my sister? Look at how much brighter and greater our God is Who lives in us (**1 John 4:4**). We aren't supposed to lay down in defeat at the sight of all the gross darkness growing around us. We are to arise with boldness in our hearts, and faithfully share the gospel. As we do, God's glory will come on us, and nations and unreached peoples will begin to come to Jesus.

John the Baptist is an example for us to see how to begin preparing the way for the second coming of the Lord. Look at **Isaiah 40:3-5** and **Matthew 3:1-3**.

> Isaiah 40:3 - "A voice of one calling: "In the desert **prepare the way** for the LORD; make straight in the wilderness **a highway** for our God.
>
> 4 Every valley shall be raised up, every mountain and hill made low; the rough ground shall become level, the rugged places a plain.
>
> 5 And the glory of the LORD will be revealed, and all mankind together will see it. For the mouth of the LORD has spoken."
>
> Matthew 3:1 - Now in those days John the Baptist *came, preaching in the wilderness of Judea, saying,
>
> 2 "Repent, for the kingdom of heaven is at hand."
>
> 3 For this is the one referred to by Isaiah the prophet when he said, "THE VOICE OF ONE CRYING IN THE WILDERNESS, '**MAKE READY THE WAY** OF THE LORD, MAKE **HIS PATHS** STRAIGHT!'"

Notice Isaiah and Matthew tell us to "prepare" and "make ready" the way of the Lord. It takes faith to do that when you might not be seeing any evidence of the harvest and glory of the Lord around you. That's when it takes faith. It took faith for John the Baptist to preach in the midst of the religious demons of his day. It took faith for Noah to preach when his family was the only God-fearing family around, and he was the laughingstock of the whole earth of his day, building a boat in the middle of nowhere! He wasn't near any body of water. Noah had a great faith in the Word of the Lord, and the signs around him. Jesus said that right before He returns, the days would be just like the days of Noah and Lot. What more evidence do you need than that! Just look around you and see the tsunami of sodomites, as well as violence and corruption filling the earth, not to mention "wars and rumors of wars" (**Matthew 24**).

Isaiah 35:4-8 also describes this highway, called the Highway of Holiness, that the Lord has called us to prepare for His coming.

> 4 Say to those with anxious heart,
> "**Take courage, fear not**.
> Behold, **your God will come with vengeance**;
> The recompense of God will come,
> **But He will save you**."
>
> 5 Then **the eyes of the blind will be opened**
> And **the ears of the deaf will be unstopped**.
>
> 6 Then **the lame will leap** like a deer,
> And **the tongue of the mute**
> **will shout** for joy.
> For waters will break forth in the wilderness
> And streams in the Arabah.

7 The scorched land will become a pool
And the thirsty ground springs of water;
In the haunt of jackals, its resting place,
Grass becomes reeds and rushes.

8 **A highway** will be there, **a roadway**,
And it will be called the **Highway of Holiness**.
The unclean will not travel on it,
But it will be for him who walks that way,
And fools will not wander on it.

The Lord is coming for a holy bride, a spotless bride, and therefore the highway is to be a holy highway. We are to especially walk in holiness during these days of darkness and moral chaos. It is in dark times when the light can be seen more clearly than ever before.

In Jesus' day there was only one prophetic voice calling, "Prepare the way for the coming of the Lord." But today there are thousands and millions of Spirit-filled Christian forerunners calling and preparing the highway of holiness for the great end-time harvest of souls and the coming of the Lord. And as we arise, the Lord's glory will begin to shine on His people more and more, and the lame will walk and the blind will see, and nations will come to the glory of His shining.

So, instead of being afraid of the future, you need to realize that we, Christians, above all people, have hope for the future. Jesus is coming back. That is our hope. He is going to renew and restore this broken and corrupted old world. He is going to purge the world of evil, war, and pain. He is going to reap a mighty harvest of souls. He is going to usher in His times of peace when He rules and reigns on the earth. That is what we are hoping for.

That is what we are longing for. This world is not our home. In this world, there is tribulation, but be of good cheer, Jesus has overcome the world (**John 16:33**)! He rose from the dead, and he is coming back for His bride, the bride of Christ!

"Lift up your head, your redemption draws near" (**Luke 21:28**).

Footnotes:

1. Examining Race, Class, and Katrina. – www.npr.org http://www.npr.org/templates/story/story.php?storyId=4850509

15

BRINGING TERROR TO THE DEVIL

"And he (the demon) begged Jesus again and again not to send them out of the area.... The demons begged Jesus..." (**Mark 5:10, 12**). NIV

I was in a meeting with leaders in China and we were talking about how to help young people. At one point one young lady began to act strangely. I realized that she was demonized. I told her to declare that Jesus was Lord and that He came in the flesh. She could not say it. Her eyes grew wide and darted from side to side, and she was looking like she was about to bolt from the room! In fact, we had to keep her from leaving. But actually it was the demon who was afraid, not really the sister. And although the demon was afraid, it didn't want to leave (come out of her). But it was struggling with being terrorized; being run out of its house. I didn't run away from it. I stared in her eyes and commanded the demon to look at me in Jesus' name. Her eyes didn't want to look at me. I commanded her to say that Jesus Christ was Lord. She would struggle to say it, but still couldn't get the words to come out of her mouth. She was demonically bound. After a few minutes of this, I stared in her eyes and commanded the demon to tell me its name. I was commanding the demon to tell me his name like Jesus said to do in certain cases. She struggled with this for a minute or so, and then, finally I saw the fearful expression leave, and her face light up. The struggle was over. Her eyes became peaceful, and then she told me her own name. I knew the demon was gone. It fled in fear. It was no longer in control. She was free. She is still free today, many years later. The demon, who before had brought fear to her life, had fled in fear from us, in Jesus' name.

There were other believers in that meeting with the sister. Some of them were a little scared, watching at a distance what was going on. Others were close by me, adding their support. Any other believer in the room that day could have done what I did and helped her get free. They just needed to know what I knew and do what I did. That is what teaching and training is all about.

All kinds of apprehensions, fears and dreads will try to hinder us in our lives if they can. God's goal for you and me is to grow up in Christ, and become who we are, overcomers, and "more than conquerors" (**Romans 8:37** KJV) through Christ. Over and over in the book of Revelation, we see the Lord say, "To him who overcomes…." (**Revelation 3:21**). This is our destiny. This is our calling. To be men and women who overcome all fears, all worries and all the works of darkness.

Now, it's a wonderful thing to conquer fear and to take back ground that the enemy has stolen from us in our lives. But as good as that is, we shouldn't stop there. God has so much more for us. He wants us to go beyond just defeating fear. He wants us to move out and take the offensive, and strike fear in the heart of the spirit of fear! Make *him* afraid. Bring fear to the devil and *his* forces. He also wants us to not just stop with a giant fear that we have defeated. Pursue the others until they are all eradicated completely, in Jesus' name! How do we do that? We do that by going forth and taking spiritual and geographic ground for God, much like Israel did when they went into their Promised Land. Remember when Israel shouted and the walls of Jericho came down? As wonderful and awesome as it was to see and experience those walls come down, they didn't stop there. Why not? The job wasn't finished. They still needed to go forward, run over those walls, and take the city! We also must not stop until every filthy spirit of fear and dread is defeated and eradicated from our lives!

Do you remember the story? When they went in to the Promised Land, Canaan, the Bible says that the people of those foreign nations were afraid of them! If Israel had any fear, which some of them probably were dealing with, they didn't let it stop them. They faced their fears and went forward. But what they didn't know and hadn't imagined was that the people in the land of Canaan *were afraid of them*. And that is actually the anointing, heritage and calling that every single Christian has, if he or she will believe it and take advantage of it.

Look at what we are told in the book of Deuteronomy.

> And command the people, saying, "You will pass through the territory of your brothers the sons of Esau who live in Seir; and **they will be afraid of you**. So be very careful; (**Deut. 2:4)**

> "So all the peoples of the earth will see that you are called by the name of the LORD, and **they will be afraid of you**. **(Deut. 28:10)**

So the Lord made clear to them that the peoples of the land of Canaan would be afraid of them! Of course, Israel had to believe what God told them, and then go forth in obedience and faith. And so it is when we walk in the fullness of the Spirit, face our fears and overcome them. Then the world will be afraid of us. In fact, that is why we face the opposition that we do in many countries of the world. In China, India, Russia and other countries, their governments and leaders of other religions are afraid the church. They make laws to keep the Bible out or under their control. They make anti-evangelism and anti-conversion laws. They make laws against healing the sick. They have seen the increase in the harvest of souls come to Jesus Christ around the world, and are afraid of Christians and Christianity. They have nothing to offer. They don't have peace, joy or the truth and justice on their side to help them. So they use violence, fear and oppression to maintain their control and power.

So with that foundation truth we saw above, God warned his people to not fear the different peoples and nations in the Promised Land, Canaan.

> **You shall not be afraid of them**; you shall well remember what the LORD your God did to Pharaoh and to all Egypt: the great trials which your eyes saw and the signs and the wonders and the mighty hand and the outstretched arm by which the LORD your God brought you out. **So shall the LORD your God do to all the peoples of whom you are afraid**. **(Deuteronomy 7:18-19)**

And in the New Testament the Lord tells us the same thing. Here we see it in the book of Philippians.

> Only conduct yourselves in a manner worthy of the gospel of Christ, so that whether I come and see you or remain absent, I will hear of you that you are standing firm in one spirit, with one mind striving together for the faith of the gospel; **in no way alarmed by your opponents**--which is **a sign of destruction for them**, **but of salvation for you**, and that too, from God.
>
> For to you it has been granted for Christ's sake, not only to believe in Him, but also to suffer for His sake, experiencing the same conflict which you saw in me, and now hear to be in me. (**Philippians 1:27-30**)

Dr. Josef Tson is a perfect example and testimony to this truth. He was a former Romanian Communist who became a Christian. He later escaped from Communist Romania, completed a Master of Divinity degree and then returned to Romania to pastor. But before he returned, Christians in America warned him not to go back. "You'll be killed," they told him. "Look, Jesus Christ was killed," he replied.

He returned to Romania and became the pastor of a very large church in Oradea. As he saw the Communists trying to stamp out Christianity, he was moved to write the ***Christian Manifesto***, criticizing the repression of the Communists. Almost immediately he was arrested and his whole library confiscated by the police.

He was interrogated every day for eight hours. One day the interrogator in charge threatened him and said, "Don't you realize I have the power to kill you?"

"Yes, I realize that," Dr. Tson replied. "But do you realize that I have the power to die?" The interrogator was shocked.

Today Dr. Tson explains his faith in this way, "Dying for the Lord is not an accident. It's not a tragedy. It's part of the job. It's part of the ministry. And it's the greatest way of preaching."

"When the secret police officer threatened to kill me, to shoot me, I smiled and I said, 'Sir, don't you understand that when you kill me you send me to glory? You cannot threaten me with glory.' He looked at me and said, 'Look, when I threaten to shoot [you] or kill [you] at least get scared. You are not normal.'"

"I'm not normal," Tson continued. "I am not natural. I am supernatural because I know that my life is only training for glory. The more suffering, the more troubles, the greater the glory." **1**

You and I aren't natural either. We are supernatural children of God. We just have to learn to walk in the calling and destiny that God has for us. Dr. Tson kept his cool under fire and persecution, and this fact struck fear and respect into the hearts of his enemies.

When we know who we are in Christ, who He is in us, and that He will never leave us or forsake us, we will not be easily alarmed or frightened by our enemies. And that fact strikes fear in the heart of the devil. Demons begin to tremble and think, "Oh no. This one isn't afraid like the others."

When Jesus went to the country of the Gerasenes, he was going into a place where others feared to tread. When you read the account from **Mark 5** it sounds like the setting of a horror story, or Edgar Allen Poe.

> They came to the other side of the sea, into the country of the Gerasenes.
> When He got out of the boat, immediately a man from the tombs with an unclean spirit met Him,
> and he had his dwelling among the tombs. And no one was able to bind him anymore, even with a chain;
> because he had often been bound with shackles and chains, and the chains had been torn apart by him and the shackles broken in pieces, and no one was strong enough to subdue him.
> Constantly, night and day, he was screaming among the tombs and in the mountains, and gashing himself with stones.
> Seeing Jesus from a distance, he ran up and bowed down before Him;
> and shouting with a loud voice, he *said, "What business do we have with each other, Jesus, Son of the Most High God? I implore You by God, do not torment me!"
> For He had been saying to him, "Come out of the man, you unclean spirit!"
> And He was asking him, "What is your name?" And he *said to Him, "My name is Legion; for we are many." (**Mark 5:1-9**)

When Jesus came on the scene these demons weren't playing around. They were used to terrorizing and scaring the fool out of anybody who might come near this man. I mean he lived in the tombs. He was always screaming and shouting and gashing himself. No one could bind him. No one knew what to do with these kinds of situations. If anyone came close to their shores they probably turned around and paddled away as fast as they could after hearing blood-curdling screams, and then seeing a naked, demonized crazy man running toward them! Then one unexpected day a boat comes across the sea to their land. And wham! Legion and his trolls were hit with a Holy Ghost shock and awe attack. The demons in this poor man were used to people departing from them, fleeing from them, fearing and running for their lives! But this time it was the demons who were falling down and begging for mercy. They were afraid of Jesus. And they will begin to fear us too when we find out who we are in Christ and start to confidently use the name of Jesus as He intended us to!

We are told in **James 4:7** to "Submit therefore to God. Resist the devil and he will flee from you." Since when does the devil flee from anyone except Jesus? Most Christians are afraid to show any boldness against the devil, fearing that he might hear them. He might attack them. Some Christians think and say, "Watch out! Don't you know that the devil might hear you?" But He's the one we want to hear it! When we know who we are, what we have and who Jesus is in us, we will obey this verse and then see the results.

The problem is that first of all, many Christians aren't very submitted to God. The first requirement for resisting the devil in this verse is to "submit therefore to God." Our authority comes from whom we are submitted to. When we are submitted to God, we show that we are under His authority. When we are under God's authority, then He commands us to resist the devil and use that authority. When we do, the devil will run in terror, with his tail between his legs. You see this verse makes it clear that we can bring terror to the devil. We can scare the devil out of the devil. We can strike fear into his heart if walk with the Lord the way He has called us to walk. Many Christians walk way below the power and authority that God has given them. That is why the devil can boss them around and intimidate them easily.

Look at how the demons responded to Jesus.

> And **they cried out**, saying, "What business do we have with each other, Son of God? Have You come here to **torment us** before the time?" (**Matthew 8:29)**

Jesus' presence and ministry felt like torment to the demons. They begged Him to leave them alone. We are the children of God. Jesus said that the same works that He did, we would do also (**John 14:12**). The devil and demons will feel the same way about our lives and ministries when we learn to walk in the Word and authority God has called us to.

The Bible says that Jesus came to destroy the works of the devil. Did you notice that? *We* destroy *his* works, not the other way around. Of course, we have to be walking in the will and Word of God. But we, like Jesus our example, are called to destroy the works of the devil, not be afraid of him or them. We first destroy his lies and thoughts in our mind, then we destroy his lies and works in others, helping to set them and nations free.

The Bible says in **Provers 28:1**, "The wicked flee when no one is pursuing, But the righteous are bold as a lion." The problem is that too many Christians are the ones fleeing when no one is pursuing. Many of the fears and apprehensions that we run from would be quickly gone if we'd just stop and face them in

Jesus' name. A sister in our church in Russia was walking down the street one night. A man began to follow her. He was getting close to her when she turned around and said, "The blood of Jesus!" The startled man stumbled backward, turned around and fled! She faced her fear in Jesus' name and it fled from her.

We have been made the righteousness of God in Christ (**2 Corinthians 5:21**). We have the boldness of a lion in us. Part of the meaning of walking in righteousness is walking by faith. The Bible says, "The righteous man shall live by faith" (**Romans 1:17**). Naturally, having faith gives us boldness. Faith in God and His promises help us to go forth and take our promised lands from the demons and giants that stand in our way.

When we know who we are, and who the enemy is, they will recognize our authority in Christ and submit to it. The demon told the seven sons of Sceva, "Paul we know, but who are you?" (**Acts 19:15**)! You are child of God also, just like Paul. When you know this, and begin to act like it's true because it is, the devil will recognize that you know who you are, and take note. He and his cohorts will think twice before considering attacking you because they know they'll probably end up running away, whipped and burned with their tails between their legs.

Proverbs 28:1 begins with, "The wicked flee." Here it says that they flee even "when no one is pursuing." We have the wrong impression of the devil and his wicked forces. We think they are brave and courageous. They are not. They are cowards. They prey upon the spiritually weak and deceived. So, surprisingly to many Christians, they are easily frightened. Granted, there are times when the devil attacks the church in a rage (**Revelation 12:12**). But my point is that we never think of them as fearful and cowing before us. So if they already tend to be easily spooked and run, what do you think they will do when the faith-filled righteous stand up to them and resist them in Jesus' name? They will flee in terror, and that with their tails between their legs!

I'm telling you, you and I are called. Our heritage is to bring terror to the devil and his demonic dogs. Look at **Luke 10:19**. "Behold, I have given you authority to tread on serpents and scorpions, and over all the power of the enemy, and nothing will injure you." We have authority over them. The problem is we haven't been taught. We haven't been trained, and therefore we rarely use the spiritual weapons and authority that we have through Jesus Christ.

We have authority to tread on them, to bring terror to them. When you step on a serpent's head, he wriggles and squirms, terrified that he is dying and there is nothing that he can do to get away. Jesus walked on serpents, scorpions, demons and devils. Serpents and scorpions represent demons. Part of walking with God is walking on demons and the works of the devil. If we walk with God we will walk on the devil and demons. Part of the Christian life and living an overcoming life is walking on devils and demons. If we walk with Jesus we will surely do this. If you don't want to walk with Jesus on this part of the path, then the serpents and scorpions will bite, sting and walk on you. It's your choice. You bring pain to them or they will bring pain to you.

One of the few animals that strike fear into snakes is an eagle. The Bible says in **Isaiah 40:31** says, "Yet those who wait for the LORD Will gain new strength; They will mount up with wings like eagles, They will run and not get tired, They will walk and not become weary." When we wait on the Lord and learn of His truth, we will gain new strength and authority. Part of that strength is likened to an eagle's. And eagles kill and eat snakes. They strike fear into snakes!

So stop and consider for a minute. Learn from the Lord who you are, and the authority and weapons that you have through Christ. You are an snake-eating eagle. Begin to walk with God over demons, serpents and scorpions. When you speak in faith the name of Jesus, when you shout praise and lift up His name, the demons begin to scream, putting their hands over their ears. They also will begin to flee in fear.

The story of Rahab the harlot brings these truths home in a very clear way. The two spies that were sent by Joshua on a reconnaissance mission ended up at the house of Rahab. Notice what she tells them.

> Now before they lay down, she came up to them on the roof, and said to the men, "I know that the LORD has given you the land, and that **the terror of you has fallen on us**, and that **all the inhabitants of the land have melted away before you**.
> "For we have heard how the LORD dried up the water of the Red Sea before you when you came out of Egypt, and what you did to the two kings of the Amorites who were beyond the Jordan, to Sihon and Og, whom you utterly destroyed.
> "When we heard it, **our hearts melted and no courage remained in any man any longer because of you**; for the LORD your God, He is God in heaven above and on earth beneath.
> (**Joshua 2:8-11**)

"The terror of you has fallen on us." There comes a time when the devil becomes afraid of us, not because of who *we* are, but because of who Jesus is in us, and that we now know the authority we have in the name of Jesus, and are using that authority to extend the kingdom of God. And they really get scared when they find out that we are blessed by God and cannot be cursed (**See Numbers 22 & 23**)! Throughout church history there have been those who have gotten a hold of these truths and were used mightily by God. Now it's our turn. It's our watch.

I mentioned before the story of David and Goliath. Let's look at that one more time (**1 Samuel 17**). David went forth to face the giant Goliath. After he killed Goliath with the sling and the stone, he didn't stop there. Look at what happened and see the results.

> And David put his hand into his bag and took from it a stone and slung it, and struck the Philistine on his forehead. And the stone sank into his forehead, so that he fell on his face to the ground.
> Thus David prevailed over the Philistine with a sling and a stone, and he struck the Philistine and killed him; but there was no sword in David's hand.
> Then David ran and stood over the Philistine and took his sword and drew it out of its sheath and killed him, **and cut off his head with it**. When the Philistines saw that their champion was dead, they fled.
> The men of Israel and Judah arose and shouted and pursued the Philistines as far as the val-

> ley, and to the gates of Ekron. And the slain Philistines lay along the way to Shaaraim, even to Gath and Ekron.
>
> The sons of Israel returned from chasing the Philistines and plundered their camps. (**1 Samuel 17:49-53**)

David used the sling and the stone. The stone is the Word of God. The sling is our mouth. We speak the Word of God, and that truth will bring down the giant fears and phobias in our lives. But David didn't stop there. He made sure the job was finished. And we need to do the same. David took Goliath's own cursed sword and cut off his head. It says that he killed him twice. He killed him with the stone and then he made sure the job was done by killing him and cutting off his head with his own cursed sword. David turned Goliath's curse words back on him. God said that He will curse those who curse us. Goliath's curse of death came back on himself. He planned to cut off David's head, but instead David cut off his head. He cut off his thoughts. He cut off his mouth and tongue so he wouldn't hear Goliath's words of fear and mocking again! And we must do the same, brothers and sisters. We must remove the head, thoughts and tongue of fear and worry, and install Jesus and his thoughts and words as King over our lives. Remove the thought patterns and words that we have become accustomed to.

The soldiers of Israel had also listened to the words of Goliath for many days. Those words had become branded in their thinking. They heard the laughs of the Philistine soldiers who responded to Goliath's mocking. They started believing those words and sat in silence. Then David removed the giant. He shut him up! But the Hebrew soldiers had to rise up and chase down the rest of the Philistine soldiers, and plunder their camps. We must do the same with thoughts and words of fears and worries that have intimidated and frozen us in our tracks. We have to stop reading, watching and listening to people and things that feed our fears instead of feed our faith. It may mean you have to stop certain relationships. It may mean you have to not watch and listen to the same movies and music you did before. All of these things are echoes of Goliath that must be eradicated and decapitated in order to complete the victory and bring terror to the devil.

Finally, another way of looking at this story is that David is a type of Jesus. He prophetically represents Jesus the Messiah who was to come. Jesus came and defeated the devil. But after David killed Goliath, the rest of the army, you and I, and all Christians worldwide, must lift up a shout of victory, pursue and destroy the rest of the army. Jesus did his part on the cross, but we must now do our part and destroy the rest of the devil's forces. Jesus has defeated the devil, and put his demonic army on the run. Let's now rise up and take back what the devil has stolen. Let's route his army and drive out every single fear, worry and dread that has come against us in our lives. Jesus is holding up Goliath's (the devil's) head. He's waiting on us to wake up, realize the victory that has been won, and join him in finishing the task before us. It's time for the tables to be turned on the devil. You no longer should be running from him, but the devil and his forces should be running from you. In fact, they are shaking in their boots as faith in this truth is rising in your heart. Put on the full armor of God. Take your stand. Run toward the terror-filled camp of the devil and command them to be gone, in Jesus' name! That is our heritage. That is who we are. Jesus wants us to be free. He has already done His part for us. Now we have our part to play in the battle. Let's take up our sling and stone, our sword and shield, and go forth to the life of freedom and victory that Jesus has called us to.

Isaiah 60:1-3 tells us

> "Arise, shine; for your light has come, And the glory of the LORD has risen upon you. For behold, darkness will cover the earth And deep darkness the peoples; But the LORD will rise upon you And His glory will appear upon you. Nations will come to your light, And kings to the brightness of your rising. "

Deep darkness may be covering the earth, but we are not to run and hide. That is not who we are! We are to "Arise and shine." In spite of Islamic terrorism, in spite of homosexual opposition and intimidation, in spite of all the forces of darkness in society clamoring for us to shut up, sit down and go away, we know that WE WERE BORN FOR SUCH A TIME AS THIS! This is our time to shine boldly and brightly for Jesus. Our "light," Christ Jesus, has come. He now lives in us and will shine through us if we don't hide Him under a bushel. God's glory is on you. Believe it, and go forth, shining in the darkness, and God's enemies will flee, new lands and peoples will be brought into the kingdom of God, and you will be fulfilling God's destiny for your life. Arise and shine, for your light has come!

Footnote:

1. (March 2 at Southern Baptist Theological Seminary in Louisville, Ky.) Posted on Jul 19, 2004 | by Jeff Robinson BIRMINGHAM, Ala. (BP) http://www.bpnews.net/18713/romanian-josef-tson-recounts-gods-grace-amid-suffering

16

INTREPIDITY AND BEYOND

Overcoming our fears in order to reach the world for Christ.

"If we wait till we run no risk, the gospel will never be introduced into the interior."
David Livingston (Missionary to Africa)

I stopped at the address near the corner of McKinley and North Simmons St. where I was scheduled to do a job for the cable company I worked for in Hollandale, MS, my hometown. As I got out of the truck, I heard a woman down the street screaming. I looked, and saw a man who had a woman by her hair and was beating her in the face over and over! Another woman was standing beside them screaming at him to stop. Immediately I looked in the back of my truck for a metal pipe to either threaten him with or hit him. But then the thought occurred to me, "If I don't get the first lick in, I'm done for. I'm in trouble." I could see that he was bigger than I was, and already in a rage. So I abandoned the pipe idea and ran over to where they were. I had heard the lady scream the man's name, so I said, "Willie! In the name of Jesus, STOP!" He didn't stop so I said it again, "Willie! In the name of Jesus, STOP!" This time he stopped! There is power in the name of Jesus! He kind of shuddered and then walked off mumbling something to himself, and then the women walked off too. Still a little stunned by the whole situation myself, but also rejoicing in the authority of the name of Jesus, I went back to my work.

Now when I first heard the woman's screams and saw what was happening, I had several choices. You may think, "Call the police," but there were no cell phones at that time. Yes, there was a time when we lived without them. This was around 1982/83. The point is, that wasn't an option.

I could also have ignored what was happening and thereby ignored the responsibility that we all have before God to protect and help the weak and those in danger. Remember, "*Do unto others as you would have them do unto you.*" But this choice, to ignore the situation, didn't even occur to me. It didn't occur to me to do nothing. My parents raised me to help people in need. So how we are raised and trained is very important. I was also raised in church to care about others.

As I already said, I could have also tried to hit him with a pipe. Now that was a viable option but I think the Holy Spirit helped me to make the right choice in this situation. But if I hadn't known of another course of action, I might have used the pipe instead.

One thing I want to mention is that I didn't have a gun. Not that I am opposed to guns at all. I come from a hunting family and several guns were passed down to me through my family (Although they were almost all stolen later.). But I'm glad that I didn't have a gun that day to fall back on because I learned a priceless spiritual lesson. The name of Jesus is more powerful than any demon of rage or any gun! I have lived all over the world and during all that time I never had a gun. I was not allowed to have a gun in those countries. Even If I was allowed, I didn't have the money to get one. We barely had enough to live on, much less buy a gun. I had to trust solely in God's protection. And that is my point and question for you. Again, not that it is wrong to have a gun. I think it's very wise to have one in most cases. But what are you trusting in? If your faith is in your gun, then you have a foundation that can be shaken. Our ultimate trust must be in God and not a gun. Shoot me as a heretic if you want to, but the Bible says, ""You come to me with a sword, a spear, and a javelin, but I come to you in the name of the LORD of hosts, the God of the armies of Israel, whom you have taunted" (**1 Samuel 17:45**). David wasn't trusting in the armor and weapons of war. He even turned down the king's armor. He wasn't trusting in his sling either. He had learned to trust in the name, protection and power of God that had helped him to kill the lion and the bear years before. And he didn't have a sword to do it with! He had learned that ultimately we have to trust in God, not our guns and armies to protect us. That's what I had to do too, first in America, and then when I moved to other countries as a missionary. Don't get me wrong. I believe we must have a strong police force, military, locks on our doors and even a gun. But the Bible says, "Some trust in chariots and some in horses, but we trust in the name of the LORD our God" (**Psalm 20:7**, ESV). Guns misfire. Armies get defeated. Terrorists blow themselves up as homicide bombers. But if your trust and faith is in God, He will never fail you. Amen! My ultimate faith is in the name of Jesus and the promises of **Psalm 91**. God is the One who can ultimately deliver us from fear and evil, not a gun.

But that day on the street I had heard of another choice besides a piece of pipe or a gun. I had heard testimonies of people using the name of Jesus in desperate situations with amazing results. And because of those testimonies and the Word of God, I followed the leading of the Lord to use the name of Jesus. So knowing that I could use the name of Jesus helped to give me confidence and courage to face that situation. It can do the same for anyone of us.

First of all, the Bible says that everyone "*who calls on the name of the Lord will be saved*" (**Acts 2:21**). This verse has to be believed and be a part of the foundation of our faith in Christ in order to give us faith and courage to face life's dangers. This calling on the name of the Lord not only relates to salvation from sin, but also salvation from dangers as well. You may think, "*Well, I know a lot of Christians that God didn't save in dangerous situations, and the apostle Paul was beaten and imprisoned.*" Well, first of all, I don't know what "*a lot of Christians*" believe. If you don't believe in **Acts 2:21** then it certainly won't work for you. We also have to remember that although Paul was beaten and suffered for Christ, Paul's own testimony was that the Lord "*delivered him out of them all*" (**2 Tim.3:11**). The times when Paul suffered these things it was for preaching the gospel. Things like that happen sometimes when we preach the gospel. But although we are called to be willing to suffer for Jesus as we preach the gospel, we don't have to submit to being robbed, murdered, or raped as might happen to some unfortunate citizen. I know of many testimonies of Christians, who when confronted by rapists, robbers, and even murderers, used the name of Jesus and saw the would-be attackers stop. The attitude of the attacker would soften, and they would end up not doing what they had planned to do. In some cases they even prayed to receive Jesus and turned themselves in!

So, meditate on this verse. Believe this verse, and grow in the confidence that we not only have in Christ's promises, but also in who we are in Christ and Who He is in us. This will help strengthen our confidence in knowing the authority we have in Christ.

Also remember **1 John 4:4**, "*Greater is he who is in us that he who is in the world.*" This verse will help us grow in faith and confidence. It will help us to face the dangerous situations that we will certainly face when we go forth in obedience to God's Word to take the gospel to those who have never heard in unreached places.

By now, you might be asking, "What does this story have to do with this chapter?" Well, Jesus told us to "*go into all the world and preach the gospel*" (**Mark 16:15**), and be witnesses of His resurrection and salvation (**Acts 1:8**). If we are ever going to reach this world for Jesus Christ, we must overcome any fear that is hindering us. We must go forth in the power and boldness of the Holy Spirit, with intrepidity, and finish the task the Lord Jesus has given us, no matter the perceived danger. He has promised to be with us, "*even to the end of the age*" (**Matthew 28:20**)! He also has promised that signs and wonders will follow us when we go forth in His name sharing the good news (**Mark 16**).

When I took my family and joined the team that was going to Nizhny Novgorod Russia in 1992 to start a church it was one of the most exciting and fulfilling times of my life. Many other teams from our mission organization later went to other cities in Russia as well. It was an awesome move of God during those days. But for me, as well as others, it was also one of the times when we had to deal with fear more than ever before. Of course, the devil didn't want us there. He knew that God was moving in an unprecedented way to open up countries and reap a mighty harvest! The Russian economy had all but fallen apart. The Russian mafia was growing by leaps and bounds. Although Russia was experiencing freedom on a scale that she hadn't experienced in at least 70 or 80 years, she was also experiencing crises that were very painful for the Russian people. People were suffering terribly and therefore many were turning to alcohol as never before. Fights and acts of violence were breaking out around us all the time. Some on our teams went through harrowing experiences where they were attacked, and others almost murdered or raped. We all could have made many excuses to not go. But by God's grace we faced our fears and went anyway. God will give us a courage and boldness beyond ourselves if we will listen and yield to His voice. Knowing that there were people praying for us and supporting us added much encouragement as well. Were we intrepid? Some called us crazy and stupid. But that's really not the right question. The most important questions is, "Are we going where the Lord wants us to go, and doing what the Lord wants us to do?" For us, the important thing was that we went in obedience to our Lord's calling and Great Commission.

But what about the next, even greater worldwide harvest that we see in the Bible (**Isaiah 60:1-3; Matthew 13:29**) and also has been prophesied by contemporary prophets? Are we going to let fears and the threat of terrorism stop us from reaping the harvest? We can't let the next harvest that comes rot in the field because we're afraid of the field or the fruit that's in it! And don't forget, the safest place you can be is in the middle of God's will.

What is intrepidity? Intrepidity is responding with resolute fearlessness in the face of extreme danger. Over and over throughout the Bible the Lord has said to us, "*Fear not*." Our lives should be characterized by resolute fearlessness. Responding like this to fear is part of our destiny as children of the Lord. We were born for such a time as this. We weren't born to be cowering somewhere, hiding from our enemy, the devil.

What is the foundation of intrepidity in the life of a Christian? Of course, it involves a strong faith in God. But it also includes caring about others more than you do about yourself. That is the heart of Jesus. He exemplified intrepidity more than any other man who has ever lived.

Now when considering overcoming our fears, many erringly feel that ignorance is bliss. Many feel that just by ignoring their fears they will go away, or nothing will happen. But that simply isn't true. The fact is that things will grow worse for you, and you won't fulfill God's plan for your life if you allow any fear to rule you. You must deal with it. The Bible says we are to "*let the peace of Christ* (not the fears of the devil) *rule in our hearts*" (**Colossians 3:15**).

We need to ask ourselves the sober question. Am I allowing any fear to hinder me from sharing Jesus with people around me? And also, a possibly even more challenging question, "Am I allowing any fear to stop me from going, either short term or long term, to share the gospel with those in other countries who have never heard the gospel?" What about in our own city in which we live?

Just like the situation I described at the beginning of this chapter, many people around the world are being beaten and abused by the devil. They don't even get a crumb from the master's table. They are kept from the knowledge of the good news of Jesus Christ. They are in deep darkness with no hope of seeing the light. If we listen carefully, we can hear their cries for help. Are we going to ignore them, or respond to the call of God, "Whom shall I send, and who will go for us" (**Isaiah 6:8**)?

There are so many stories of people who, because of fear, refused to help others who were in trouble, injured and calling for help. We need to take a sober, hard look at ourselves and our lives. What are we doing for Jesus? Is our life making a difference in the world? Jesus told a story we call the Good Samaritan. As the story goes, there was a man lying on the side of the road who had been beaten and robbed by thieves. A priest, considered to be a holy man of Israel, saw him and passed by. He did nothing. Then another holy man of Israel, a Levite, passed by. He also did nothing to help the man. They were too busy, too afraid, or too selfish to get involved. How about us? What is our excuse? If we aren't too busy or selfish, the devil will try to bind us with fears. That way he can keep us from leaving our houses, flying in airplanes, going to where the hurting, crying, lost and dying people are found.

On October 13, 2011, in an alley way in one of the open markets of Foshan City, Guangdong, China, a little two-year-old girl named Wang YueYue was accidently struck and run over by a small van as she walked back to her parents' shop. But the driver didn't stop to check and see what he'd hit. Even more shocking, seeing the video footage, you can count 16 people who passed by her little, unconscious body and did nothing (Like the Levite and Priest in the story of the Good Samaritan). Unbelievably, another vehicle came through a few minutes later and ran over her a second time! No one would stop and check on her well-being! Finally, an elderly lady, Chen Xianmei, who picks up scraps of junk cloth to sell and make a living, stopped to help the little girl and called out for help. Yue Yue's mother finally heard what had happened and came running over and rushed her daughter to the hospital. But it was too late. She died soon after. People in the video were identified and questioned. Several felt guilty and had remorse because of their callousness, and unwillingness to check on an injured child. 1

My point is, and God's will for you and I is, to not let fears and worries hinder or stop us from fulfilling God's will for our lives. Each one of us must do our part to help those in need around us, as well as see a lost world reached for Christ.

Years ago, evangelist Arthur Blessitt had a ministry on Sunset Strip in California called His Place. It was a Christian coffee house type of ministry where they had music, messages and served free snacks to the young people wandering up and down the strip. Rough people, from Hell's Angels motorcycle gang members to pimps, prostitutes, and drug pushers would also show up from time to time to hang out. One day Arthur got a call from an elderly lady, named Mrs. Bean, who wanted to help. She offered to come and do what she could to reach the young people there. Arthur appreciated her compassion but initially felt it wasn't the best place for her to be. But she was insistent and wouldn't give up. Finally, Arthur said, "Why don't you bake some pies? We serve food to the young people. So why don't you make some pies, bring the pies and we'll serve them?"

She showed up with loads of pies. They usually just put the food out, and the young people would come and grab it, but Mrs. Bean brought little plates and forks. She set it all up nicely. And when the big, dirty biker guys came up she'd say, "Look at you. You ought to be ashamed of yourself! Filthy, dirty, living like you are. You need to give your life to Jesus. He loves you and died for you!" Arthur was amazed to see guy after and guy and girl after girl that Mrs. Bean led to the Lord.

Mrs. Bean didn't look very impressive at all. What gave her the courage and intrepidity to minister among Hell's Angels and motorcycle gangs? She knew God and she had compassion. She heard the call of the Lord, and made herself available. Many are called, but few answer the call. Many are probably much more gifted and qualified, but they aren't available and don't show up! Mrs. Bean showed up! Rise up, my brother and sister! "Greater is He who is in you than He who is in the world" (**1 John 4:4**). You can do all things through Christ who strengthens you (**Philippians 4:13**). Keep your eyes on Jesus. Focus on His Word and His heart of compassion that He has put within you. You'll soon find that you are like Peter, walking on the water and doing things that you never dreamed you would do. You are walking with Jesus, shining your light in a lost and dying world.

What else can we do to keep from being like those who ignored little Yue Yue, and instead follow the example of the intrepid Mrs. Bean? Ask yourself the question, "Why am I here? What does God want me to do to reach a lost and dying world?" Allow God to touch and move your heart. The Bible says in **Matthew 24:12** that in the last days, "*Because lawlessness is increased, most people's love will grow cold.*" But this doesn't mean that everybody's heart has to grow cold. Your heart and mine don't have to grow cold.

But how can we keep our hearts burning for God, with love and compassion toward people who don't know Jesus? How can we overcome the fears, dangers and terrors in the world today that seek to neuter us from being the fearless men and women of God we are called to be, who do not fear for their lives even when faced with death (**Revelations 12:11**)? To further answer that question I think it will help to look at the citation given to those soldiers in the American military who receive the Congressional Medal of Honor. This medal is the highest honor that a soldier in combat can receive for bravery. When a soldier receives the Medal of Honor, the citation usually reads, "*For conspicuous* *gallantry and intrepidity at the risk of life above and beyond the call of duty*." It doesn't just say "gallantry and intrepidity." It says "conspicuous" gallantry and intrepidity. Those two without any adjective would be very good in themselves. Most soldiers in combat are already showing gallantry and intrepidity. But this medal is only given when *special* and *outstanding* gallantry and intrepidity are shown in combat.

Gallantry and intrepidity aren't words that we are very familiar with these days. We don't use them much anymore. They seem to be words more from days gone by than the days that we are living in. And that's the problem. If a young person heard these words, they would more than likely think of some movie action hero or a sports superstar. True heroes aren't usually honored and lauded as they should be in our generation. To be sure, there are shining examples for us today, but we need to realize that you and I are also all called to step forward and say, "Here am I, Lord. Send me. I'll go where you want me to go. I'll do what you want me to do." But more often we hear, "Here am I, send them!" What can we do to change this? Studying the examples of true heroes can inspire us to rise above the status quo and the average lifestyle that many are accustomed to.

Gallantry means conspicuous, courageous behavior, especially in battle. As I've already said, we all must realize that we are in a spiritual battle. Satan and his demonic forces hate you and desire to destroy your life, marriage and children. We must wake up. Get in the battle. Get involved with helping others come to know Jesus.

In the book "Joker Five" about a Marine squad that was deployed in a very dangerous city of Iraq, there was one soldier in their platoon that was narcoleptic. He could fall asleep in almost any situation, even in tense and dangerous ones. The church today seems to have the same condition. She is in a narcoleptic sleep. And the Lord is sounding the alarm to wake up and get ready for battle! Get in the battle! Our freedoms are being stolen from us one by one, and the world without Jesus is going to hell. But we are like some narcoleptic Jonah, asleep in the storm, running from God, while the lost heathen are crying out to their gods for help! What did it take to wake up Jonah? It took a storm and lost heathens to wake him up. And that is what is happening today. Storms are shaking and rocking our boat, and the Lord is using the brazen attacks of atheists, homosexuals, terrorists, communists and economic earthquakes to shake and wake the church out of her stupor. Didn't Jesus say to "*be on the alert, for you do not know which day your Lord is coming*" (**Mt.24:42**). In verse 44 He said, "*...You also must be ready.*" Most of us aren't alert and we aren't ready either. It's past time to wake up, get ready and into action.

As I mentioned above, intrepidity refers to acts that are characterized by resolute fearlessness. Of course, there are many examples we could find in the Bible. But let's look at Gideon. We might be able to relate to him a little easier. Many of us are like Gideon. We need a revelation of who we are and a renewing in our minds of our self-image in Christ. Remember when the angel appeared to Gideon? He said, "*The Lord is with you, O valiant warrior*" (**Judges 6:12**). Gideon was probably looking around and thinking, "Who is this guy talking to? I'm here in the wine press, secretly beating out wheat so it doesn't get stolen by the Midianites. And where are all of God's miracles they told us about? It seems to me that he Lord has abandoned us." Gideon had drifted so far from the Lord that He no longer realized that the Lord was with him. He also didn't see himself the way God saw him, and he didn't think or declare to himself the things that

God thought and said about him. We need a renewed mind that **Romans 12:2** talks about. We need to believe, think and profess about ourselves what God says. We should agree with God, not dispute what He is saying. Not believing the good things God says about us is part of what keeps us in the Gideon/Midianite syndrome. Well, thank God He is sending angels, situations, and even using the heathen to wake us up, and get us back into training and the battle. Gideon ultimately listened to the Lord, and in spite of his reluctance and struggle with fear, was able to bring about a great victory for the Lord and His people. We too can grow and be used of the Lord as well.

Continuing to look at the citation for the Medal of Honor, it follows with the phrase, "*At the risk of life.*" This seems to be a big part of what it means to follow Jesus Christ, to believe His promises, and act on them. Thankfully, most of us don't live in constant danger and risk of our lives, but there are times that we end up in risky or life-threatening situations whether we are ready or not. Knowing the Lord and His promises is extremely important in times like that. But that's not what I'm talking about here. Here we are talking about people *choosing* to go into either potentially threatening places and situations, or places that you know are already dangerous and life threatening in one way or another.

Almost anywhere in the world, even in relatively safe countries or cities, there are places or parts of cities that people try to avoid because of the danger or violence characterized by that place. But there are some courageous Christians who hear the call of God, and purposely go into places like that to share the gospel. Some even choose to live in such places.

Throughout history there have been Christians who have gone to countries that were riddled with diseases and tribes of cannibals. And some of them did die serving the Lord, or were martyred for their faith. Others lived to tell the story of how God protected them, delivered them, and worked mighty miracles among them. They are part of God's honor roll. Many of them we could call recipients of God's Medal of Honor.

In the Bible we could look at the eleventh chapter of the book of Hebrews for such a list of intrepid people. Of course, the main theme of that chapter is faith, and how it is through faith that we please God. And also, faith is certainly an ingredient that makes up courage, especially Christian courage. It is faith that helps give us the courage to do the things that God has called us to do. Now, we don't normally start out being gallant and courageous. In fact, we start out clinging to our mama and daddy. But as we grow in a proper environment, we develop security, confidence, and even a measure of courage to do certain things.

If you have a family, hopefully all of you would be willing to die for your spouse and your children. You would give your life in order to save them. But even though we don't all start out courageous, we can grow in faith, courage, bravery, and intrepidity. In fact, it is God's will for us to grow in these qualities. If we aren't growing in these qualities, we aren't pleasing to God. And if its God's will that we are growing in faith and courage, but we aren't, then we aren't only non-pleasing to God, which is bad enough, but we are in sin as well.

In 2008, there was a terrible earthquake in Sichuan Province, China. It registered 7.9 on the Richter scale and over 86,000 died. During that earthquake many children in elementary schools died because the builders used building materials below the required specifications. They bought the cheaper materials and then pocketed the extra money that was allocated for the more expensive materials. So when the earthquake hit, the buildings quickly collapsed before the children could escape.

In one school in particular, it was discovered that one teacher, Fan Meizhong, made it out but he had left all of his children inside. Thankfully and incredibly they all made it out alive! He had instructed the children to crawl under their desks but then he left them and ran outside.

When asked how he could do such a thing he replied, "I ran towards the stairs so fast that I stumbled and fell as I went. When I reached the center of the football field, I found I was the first to escape. None of my pupils were with me," wrote the man now known across China as 'Runner Fan'.

When his pupils began to arrive, they asked: "Teacher, why didn't you lead us out?" His explanation was simple. "I have a very strong sense of self-preservation," he said. "I have never been a brave man and I'm only really concerned about myself." "I didn't cause the earthquake, so I have no reason to feel guilty," he said in an interview. "When I got back to the classroom, the students were all fine." He also risked angering those closer to him, saying he would not have tried to save his own mother if she had been present, though he *might* have made an exception to his general rule for his one-year-old daughter!

Many news reports focused on stories of most teachers putting children first, as we would expect. One of those teachers was Tan Qianqiu, whose body was found shielding four of his pupils, all of them alive.

But some schools were uneasy that their teachers had a higher survival rate compared to pupils. One such school was the Juyuan School. Hundreds of students died there. Parents say 500 to 700 died, although the "official" number was 278 out of 900. But only six out of eighty teachers died! Parents pointed out that teachers stood nearest to the doors of the classrooms, so they were able to escape quickly.

Finally, the cowardly teacher, Fan Meizhong, pointed out that education law did not demand that a teacher save his pupils during an earthquake. "If every teacher was like Mr. Tan (who gave his life for his students), then we'd have no more heroes," he said. "I admire heroes like Mr. Tan, but I can't do that myself. I love my life more." 2

Hopefully, we would all be like the teacher, Mr. Tan. But whether we feel that way or not, the good news is that we can grow in faith and we can grow in courage to the point that we are doing things that we never dreamed we would do. I for one, have experienced such a transformation since knowing the Lord, and by His grace, have done things that, without Him, I never would have or could have done.

One moving example of Christian gallantry and intrepidity was on October 29, 2009, in Pakistan. A lowly, Christian janitor, Pervaiz Masih, was working at Islamabad's International Islamic University. He had only been at work there for one week when an Islamic homicide bomber worked his way into the women's side of the campus. The terrorist had already shot a guard and was trying to enter his target destination, the cafeteria where 300 to 400 women students were gathered for their meal.

Why would a Muslim want to murder fellow Muslims, especially women? Such is the twisted doctrine of Islam. It rabidly wants to keep women enslaved to Islamic men to such a degree that it is willing to use terror and murder to keep them from getting an education. An education poses a threat to many Islamic men and their interpretation of the Koran, as well as the life of Mohammed.

So as the terrorist was fast approaching his goal, he had no idea what was about to happen. Pervaiz Masih saw him coming, stepped out of the doorway of the cafeteria and confronted him. Masih is a common name among the Christian minority in Pakistan. It means Messiah. And Masih certainly followed in the footsteps of his Messiah, Jesus, that day. He refused to let the bomber pass. In the process the bomb detonated, killing Masih, the bomber, and three girls nearby.

Meanwhile, inside the cafeteria, the 300 to 400 Muslim girls were unharmed. But two martyrs lay in the midst of the rubble. One was a so-called Muslim "martyr" who murdered others. The other was a Christian martyr who laid down his life to save others. Masih, a Christian, died to save Muslims from a fellow Muslim.

Masih left behind his wife, a three year old daughter, named Diya, and elderly parents. They had to borrow money to buy a coffin for him. His body initially lay in a garbage-strewn cemetery beside a mud road. Thankfully the government afterward did build a much more honorable gravesite and stone for him. They also have provided money for his family.

Professor Fateh Muhammad Malik, a rector of the university said that Pervaiz Masih "*rose above the barriers of caste, creed, and sectarian terrorism. Despite being a Christian, he sacrificed his life to save the Muslim girls*." But Professor Malik was mistaken on one point. It wasn't "*despite*" his being a Christian that Pervaiz did what he did, but instead, ***because*** he was a Christian he faced the terrorist, and laid down his own life. 3

And again, the amazing thing is that he laid down his life for Muslims. In my mind, I can picture Heaven presenting to Pervaiz Masih the Heavenly Medal of Honor. "To Pervaiz Masih, for conspicuous gallantry and intrepidity at the risk of life above and beyond the call of duty." I look forward to meeting him in Heaven one day. He is one of Heaven's heroes that we should desire to emulate.

You may feel like Corrie Ten Boom did when she was a little girl. She tells the story in her book "Tramp for the Lord." She said, "Daddy, I am afraid that I will never be strong enough to be a martyr for Jesus Christ." "Tell me,' her father said, 'when you take a train trip from Haarlem to Amsterdam, when do I give you the money for the ticket? Three weeks before?' "No Daddy, you give me the money for the ticket just before we get on the train.' "That is right.' My father said, 'and so it is with God's strength. Our wise Father in heaven knows when you are going to need things too. Today you do not need the strength to be a martyr; but as soon as you are called upon for the honor of facing death for Jesus, He will supply the strength you need --- just in time.' Later in life Corrie testified, "I took great comfort in my father's advice. Later I had to suffer for Jesus in a concentration camp. He indeed gave me all the courage and power I needed."(4) So we do our part to grow in Christ, but we also must walk by faith and trust the Lord to give us the grace to do what we need when the situation warrants it, and we are persecuted for Christ.

Joshua was a man who found himself in a similar situation in which we, the church of Jesus Christ, find ourselves today. The generation before Joshua had failed to take the Promised Land that God had called them to take. Now, Joshua and the people of Israel found themselves in the exact place where the previous generation had come to and failed. They were facing the same challenges, cities, and giants. What were they going to do? We also face a world, a promised land if you will, that the Lord has told us to go forth and reach for Jesus Christ. The previous generation to Joshua died in the wilderness because of their fear and unbelief. What are we going to do in our generation? We would do well to heed the words the Lord spoke to him as he was standing on the precipice of divine destiny. Look at **Joshua1:6-9**.

> "**Be strong and courageous**, for you shall give this people possession of the land which I swore to their fathers to give them.
> "Only **be strong and very courageous**; be careful to do according to all the law which Moses My servant commanded you; do not turn from it to the right or to the left, so that you may have success wherever you go.
> "Have I not commanded you? **Be strong and courageous**! Do not tremble or be dismayed, for the LORD your God is with you wherever you go."

My friends, Joshua lived under the Old Covenant. We live under the New. We have greater promises than what they had. We have a better, greater covenant than they had. God is for us and lives in us, and has told us that He also will never leave us or forsake us. He will be with us to the end of the age! We must work together to go forward to take not only the cities and neighborhoods where we live, but also the promised lands of unreached peoples. They are the ones throughout the world today who have never heard of Jesus Christ. While we are longing for His second coming, they are still waiting to hear about the first!

Read and meditate on those words spoken to Joshua. His taking the Promised Land is an example and metaphor of two things for us. It is, first of all, a type of our having a victorious Christian life. We all have a "land" to take, filled with blessings and promises from the Lord. But the other thing that this symbolizes for us is our challenge to take the world for Jesus Christ. God is telling us exactly what He told Joshua. "Be strong and courageous!" Go forward and take the lands, the nations for my Son, who gave His life for them. Take the Good News into the whole world, to every nation and people group. "Only be strong and courageous!" And then, the third time, for even greater emphasis, He says, "Have I not commanded you? Be strong and courageous! Do not tremble or be dismayed." That is awesome in itself, but the ending is even better. He states, "For the Lord your God is with you wherever you go." Amen! Hallelujah! Do you believe that? We need to meditate on this until the truth of it gets down into our spirits, our hearts, where faith is born. Then we'll rise up like the spiritual army we are called to be, going forth doing exploits for God.

Here are some action steps that we can take to grow in courage, intrepidity, and grace for going not only into the streets and city around us, but even to the remotest parts of the world.

1. Practice thinking about others more than yourself! If you are going to love your neighbor, then you have to think about them and not just yourself, especially if they are lost. Of course, our neighbors, who have never heard of Jesus, are in other countries also. **Philippians 2:4** says, "*Do not merely look out for your own personal interests, but also for the interests of others.*"
2. Have as your role models, your heroes, those who put others first, and care for the defenseless, weak, and poor.
3. Grow in the love and fear of God. We must realize that the Lord will hold each of us personally responsible for reach-

ing the world for Jesus. No, we can't go everywhere, but we can and must go to those to whom Jesus is calling us, whether that is across the street from us or across the ocean to another country.

4. Open your eyes. Get a vision. Allow love and compassion to grow in your heart. David Wilkerson saw a gang of young people from the streets of New York on trial for murder. The love of Christ and the leading of the Holy Spirit welled up within his heart. He could have tried to ignore it. He could have closed his eyes or looked the other way. But he decided to listen to the Lord, listen to the love and compassion of God and then take the next step to get involved. You can read about his life experience in the book, "The Cross and the Switchblade." The point is that he went to New York and trusted God to guide him and show him what to do. Was there a chance of getting hurt? Yes, of course. But love is willing to take that chance. Love can empower us to act with intrepidity. Jesus was willing and He is calling us to come follow Him into a lost and dying world. David Wilkerson, like Jesus, did his part, and trusted God to do His part as well. As a result, many youths from the gangs in New York were saved, including Nicky Cruz, the most infamous gang leader, who ended up becoming a powerful evangelist.
5. Pray for the lost. Also pray and ask God how you can get involved in the harvest yourself. Ask the Lord how you can be a part of reaching the lost not only in your city, state, and country, but also to those in other lands who have never heard of Jesus even once.
6. Ask the Lord to baptize you and fill you with His Holy Spirit. The disciples were timid and fearful until they were baptized, filled, and then learned to keep getting refilled

with the Holy Spirit on a regular basis. We are foolish to think we can win the world without the daily and fresh anointing of the Holy Spirit. Along with this, pray in your supernatural prayer language every day like Jude 20, 21 tells us. "But you, beloved, building yourselves up on your most holy faith, praying in the Holy Spirit, keep yourselves in the love of God,.."

7. Meditate on the Scriptures that speak of reaching the lost and those in darkness who have never heard of Jesus. The Bible says, "Blessed are the merciful, for they will receive mercy." If you want mercy, then, according to God, you better show mercy to others, and especially to those who have never heard of Jesus Christ.

Footnotes:

1. Video footage at this web address. Warning. Graphic. https://www.youtube.com/watch?v=ULaZhM2XLYo
2. (By Richard Spencer in Beijing 12:20PM BST 02 Jun 2008 http://www.telegraph.co.uk/news/worldnews/asia/china/2064945/China-earthquake-Teacher-admits-leaving-pupils-behind-as-he-fled-Chinese-earthquake.html)
3. Pervez Masih http://edition.cnn.com/2009/WORLD/asiapcf/11/11/pakistan.hero/
4. "Tramp for the Lord" © 1974 – By Corrie Ten Boom and Jamie Buckingham. Page 117.